Walter Savage's
WROXTON
Journals

*With a Foreword by Dr. Nicholas Baldwin, Dean of Wroxton
College, and an Introduction by Dr. Walter Cummins*

FAIRLEIGH DICKINSON UNIVERSITY
OFFICE OF GLOBAL LEARNING

NEW JERSEY

Copyright © 2009 Walter Savage
Foreword copyright © 2009 Fairleigh Dickinson University
Introduction copyright © 2009 Fairleigh Dickinson University

All Rights Reserved.

Editors: Walter Cummins and Jason Scorza
Production & Design: Mahesh Nair
Photo credits:
Rev. Thomas Shaklin (for photos from 1966-67)
Art Petrosemolo, Dan Landau, and FDU Photo Archives
Walter Cummins
William R. Kennedy
Monica Carsky

Distributed by Fairleigh Dickinson University
Published by The Office of Global Learning

Dedicated to the Wroxton students who have become such loyal friends

- Walter Savage

Foreword

I first met Walter Savage in the early Spring of 1985; I had joined the faculty at Wroxton College the previous summer as Lecturer and Tutor in British Government and Politics and was in this position when the then Head of the College was given a sabbatical and the University sent Walter over to Wroxton to coordinate the 1985 Spring Semester group and programme. Wroxton was not 'new' to Walter as he had been in charge of the College during the Spring and Fall Semesters of 1967. In 1985 I was a faculty member in residence, living in the Abbey itself; Walter came and resided in the Abbey also. As a result of these arrangements – for those who do not know Wroxton it is a small residential tutorial-based College where those in residence are in close proximity to each other – Walter and I got to know each other very well over the ensuing 15 weeks.

At the end of the Semester Walter returned to the United States and I returned to my family home some 170 miles away from Wroxton. A couple of days later I received a phone call from Walter telling me that the Head of the College had in fact resigned and that he – Walter – was returning to Wroxton to organise and co-ordinate the various summer programmes. He also asked me if I would be able to teach for him at the College that summer – to which I replied that I would be happy to do so. Walter then asked me if I could possibly do him a favour. I knew something was afoot as you could tell by the way that he was that he would have had a twinkle in his eye. I replied that I would certainly do what I could. He then asked me if I would be willing to take over from him as acting head of the College following the summer programmes. I believe I said "let me think about it yes"! Consequently, on the 1st of August 1985 Walter Savage handed over to me as head of the College.

As, more than 24 years later, I am still at Wroxton it should be apparent that I owe Walter a great deal; it is evident that my life would have taken a very different turn if it had not been for Walter Savage.

W roxton – the College; the Abbey; the Estate – is a very special – even magical – place. When seen through the eyes – and experienced through the words of Walter Savage – it was – and is – impossible not to fall in love with it.

INTRODUCTION

Why? Well, Walter was something of a cross between the late George Burns, one of Dickens' most colourful characters and Hans Christian Anderson. Larger than life, humorous, erudite, a font of knowledge on a wide variety of topics, wonderful company, thoughtful, as honest as the day is long, fair, committed, principled with a razor-sharp intellect and someone who appreciated history, tradition, nature and the importance of people. Indeed, these were all facets that were evident in the man, not least of all during his time at Wroxton.

To spend time in Walter's company was to see life through very observant eyes, for he had the ability to make even the ordinary extraordinary – for when he recounted events they became extraordinary. For example, I remember on one occasion driving out and about with Walter in my – at the time very ancient – car when, in the middle of a remote village, the vehicle broke down. We walked to the local pub and asked if we could use the phone to call for assistance – only to find that the only other person in the place was a qualified mechanic for the very type of car concerned and that he just happened to have his tool box with him. If nothing else, it was something of a coincidence; to hear Walter recount the story was to fully appreciate the art of storytelling.

Similarly, to hear Walter recount a trip (in the same vehicle) when first he, then – under his direction – both my Mother and then my Grandmother – all ended up having to get out and push the car up an increasingly steep hill, was not merely to appreciate an extensive vocabulary but how to use words to weave a picture and create a lasting imagine in the mind; and to do so while ensuring a lasting smile.

In short, Walter could certainly tell a story. Indeed, he had the ability to make even the phone book sound interesting! Walters's experiences at Wroxton, of the place and the people, have been a rich seam for his stories. Indeed, having Walter recount his Wroxton adventures was – as I have said – to experience the art of story-telling at its very best.

All that was required was to pull up a chair, relax, and let Walter paint you a picture. He was a remarkable individual and I for one will miss his wise council, his insightful observations, his humanity and above all his friendship. Indeed, I count myself as fortunate to have been able to call Walter 'friend'.

DR. NICHOLAS DJ BALDWIN
DEAN AND DIRECTOR OF OPERATIONS
WROXTON COLLEGE
FAIRLEIGH DICKINSON UNIVERSITY

Introduction

Walter Savage's great affection for Wroxton College, Wroxton village, the English countryside, and English lore and eccentricities enlivens every page of these journals. He makes the happenings of two and four decades ago immediate and vivid as he moves through the hallways of the Abbey, walks about the grounds, engages with the locals, and visits nearby towns. He is constantly observant, often amused by what he sees and experiences – a sign on a wall, a passage in a book, a glimpse of bizarre behavior, a snatch of conversation. But ultimately, he is moved by his experiences.

Although Savage's ear and eye for the odd and the comic inform all of his writing, the prevalence of such details make the emotional moments even more effective. He has too much of a grounding in 18th century wit and satire, the world of Pope and Swift, to fall into easy sentimentality and write a gushing paean to Wroxton. But there is no doubt he loves the place.

Here is Savage in his very first journal entry of 13 August 1966, "hauled by Dean Haberly out to the freshly excavated sewer trench that has been giving clues to some of the Abbey's past." Before a cup of coffee he is "sloshing around in a ditch nine feet deep and mucky from yesterday's heavy rains." Yet looking into that ditch, he sees "unearthed skeletons, roof and floor tiles, mullions, bits of stained glass, great silver headed nails, and broken sections of intricately carved columns, capitals, and bosses. Many of the fragments are brightened by splashes of gold, red, or blue paint." And he feels "slightly eerie seeing the colors shining in the sun."

These few sentences encapsulate the character of the entire journal – Savage, bemused by the situation he has gotten himself into, fascinated by all that he witnesses, and awed by his presence amidst so many centuries of history.

For the reader, beyond all that we learn about Wroxton and its environs, the greatest joy is the skill and wit of Savage's telling. No one else could describe the nature of a meal like this: "a typical Wroxton one in that the bacon was strikingly like what I imagine uncooked ear lobe would be and the fried eggs featured yolks the consistency of Turkish taffy and whites floating in oleaginous puddles." Nor could anyone else evoke the striking beauty of the Abbey like this: "I suppose that all of us years from now will find those contented moments coming back to us with a sweet sort of melancholy full of the lovely and yet softly sad colors of the sky above the Abbey's great gables, gray purples and pinks faintly gilded. I am sure that I will."

These journals are quite wonderful, and it is a great pleasure to see them in print for many to share. For those who know Wroxton, they will revive and enrich memories. For those who have not yet had the pleasure of a stay, they will instill a longing to share in such a rich environment. We can all be thankful that Walter Savage took the time to write them.

DR. WALTER CUMMINS
EMERITUS PROFESSOR OF ENGLISH
FAIRLEIGH DICKINSON UNIVERSITY

Dean Haberly leading the procession through Wroxton Village to honor the founding of the College

Wroxton students off-campus on an archeological dig with Dr. Henry Wright Baker (standing in pit), the scholar who successfully unrolled The Dead Sea Scrolls

1966

13 August 1966

The last day and a half at the Abbey has been in many ways remarkable, in some respects unbelievable, in its juxtaposings of contentment and melancholy, delights and shocks, order and Chaplinesque chaos.

The whole business began early yesterday morning. Before breakfast I was hauled by Dean Haberly out to the freshly excavated sewer trench that has been giving clues to some of the Abbey's past. The shovels and scoops have unearthed skeletons, roof and floor tiles, mullions, bits of stained glass, great silver headed nails, and broken sections of intricately carved columns, capitals, and bosses. Many of the fragments are brightened by splashes of gold, red, or blue paint. I felt slightly eerie seeing the colors shining in the sun, many hundreds of years after it was applied, perhaps, by the Augustinian monks who built their church and priory here long before the place was to know the Raynesfords, the Popes, and the Norths who were later to own it successively.

The Dean, who was at the very point of departing when he led me out to the trench, had two objectives for our pre-breakfast trip. He wanted to scratch at the trench sides for more of the red floor tiles he had been finding daily, and he wanted to alert me to watch for the back hoe's uncovering of more of the church walls, first broken into a day or so before. His interest in the precise location of the latter had become so keen that, wearied as he was by his long and tiring duties with the summer graduate program, he was about to postpone his departure so that he could stay with the digging.

Before we had so much as a sip of juice or coffee, therefore, we were sloshing around in a ditch nine feet deep and mucky from yesterday's heavy rains. His passion and my compliance—though it became more than that, for his wonderful enthusiasm, like his fluting laughter, is contagious—were quickly rewarded. Both of us uncovered a tile. His was broken, but large, with a fine deep gold pattern on its glazed terra cotta background—a cross, a fleur de lis, and a pine tree. It was striking. Mine was intact, but small, about two and a half inches square. It was a bold Lombardic Z, with a line drawn horizontally through its center. The Dean was hot on the scent and wanted to go on, but the rain, which began suddenly, and the reverberating Wroxton breakfast gong hurried us into the dining room.

Our meal was soon over, for the Haberlys had to rush out to a taxi at 8:10. Like all those we had together, however, it was a pleasant one. I have never met a man with such lively and unfailing good humor. Reminiscence after reminiscence tumbles out of him, each one a joy. Over hasty swallows of breakfast coffee, he can somehow be reminded of, and able to recapture in sprightly terms, the delightful oddities he has encountered in his uncommonly unconventional experience.

    One of them is about his having awakened years ago to find a large bat in the shirt of his pajamas. A second deals with his once having attended a recital by a flautist whose plastic artificial eye exploded from its socket in the middle of his rendition of a 16th century composition. A third concerns his having visited a children's school run by a Miss Maypother, who made her students live the stages of civilization (dressing, for instance, at first in hides and finally in contemporary clothes) and had all doorways three feet high so that adults had to crawl through them. A fourth recalls his having been commissioned to bind, illustrate, and print, for a wealthy eccentric woman (a Schwab heiress) a book written in a language of her own invention. She wanted the text in gold on lavender vellum, and she ordered him, for as long as he worked, to stay in one room of her home so that he would not shock her recently bereaved male cockatoo, mortally vulnerable, since the death of his mate, to the sudden appearance of any man.

    He can also draw upon his vast reading and study—and a memory that must be photographic—to respond with lectures in miniature to questions about stained glass, Roman Britain, the structure and regimen of monasteries, literary figures with whom he has had close associations, and an almost awe inspiring range of other subjects. All that he says he says well and with a modesty that seems altogether unnecessary.

I have frequently asked him to allow me to tape at least a few of the memories he shares with listeners, but he steadfastly refuses. "No, no, no, Savage," he tells me with dismissive shakings of his raised hands. "Never." When I protest and ask him why, he says, "Because I improve each of them with every telling."

As they are, the stories need no refining. They are so good, in fact, that several of the lecturers who visit Wroxton's classes regularly have told me that one of the principal attractions of the place is the opportunity to hear the Dean recall some of the events of his past. Stanley Wells, for one, has more than once told me that he would probably give his lectures here without an honorarium if, on each of his visits, he could be sure that he could enjoy some of Haberly's anecdotes.

We said goodbye to the Dean and Mrs. Haberly with honest sadness. We knew that we would miss them both. We knew, also, that we would now be almost totally alone in the vast and creaky building, for no students were expected until September 5.

I was especially loath to give up not only the Dean's conversation but also his infectious curiosity and capacity for observation which had made my every walk with him about the Abbey grounds, every poking into garrets and little used rooms an adventure and a discovery.

As an example, he noticed that two windows in the Great Hall, facing the Minstrels' Gallery, are so mullioned and leaded that they must once have been outside windows. The observation led him to the conclusion that the center of the building, assumed for a hundred years to be the oldest part of the Abbey, must postdate the rest of the structure. The discovery was made apparently, simply as he strolled along. I learned later that his speculation was probably wrong. In this instance as in every other one I knew of, however, he was, in his ceaselessly zestful spirit of exploration, always in the right.

After the Haberlys departed, our day was, surprisingly, pleasant and easy until 2:00 p.m. We bustled about with letters and memos and semester planning and walked through the charming village just outside the College gates. We watched a workman thatching a roof, stopped in at Mrs. Friend's small gift shop, and introduced ourselves to Mrs. Scott (who runs the tiny grocery store) and to Mrs. Jessie Cook, "licensed to sell beer to be consumed off the premises" and Wroxton's singularly friendly postmistress, perhaps the only postmistress or postmaster who licks and applies for you whatever stamps you purchase from her in the little cubicle just off the hallway of her and her family's living quarters.

At 2:00 p.m., however, I got a call from Dr. Stanley Wells, who invited us to a dinner conference at the Black Swan, or "Dirty Duck," in Stratford at 6:30. I accepted hastily, for the atmosphere of the deserted Abbey closes in on one quickly and, besides, Wells and I had to shape up the first four weeks of the Shakespeare course. Right then, Patty's and my troubles began, although I did not know so at the time.

My inquiry to the Midland Red Bus Company offered no cause for alarm. The woman who took my call quickly told me that a bus left for Stratford from Banbury, at the Cross, at 6:03 and arrived in Stratford at 7:00. I had, of course, to call Dr. Wells and ask for a half hour's grace, but there was no real problem about that or about getting by taxi to Banbury, which we reached at 5:30. Our driver began our difficulty. He told us that the bus left from the depot, not from the Cross, and therefore took us to that place, about 9 blocks from the Cross. After idling for two or three minutes, I grew uneasy and began to ask around about the exact point of departure. Five different bus drivers gave me five conflicting sets of instructions. They agreed on only one point: the bus information booth was closed.

Sifting the varying directions, Patty and I decided that the Cross was the safest waiting place after all, and at about 5:40 we started out briskly in a beginning shower. After only a block Patty became a virtual cripple. The rain, the damp pavements, and her high heels did something excruciating to a toe she broke years before. We would walk twenty steps and stop, she leaning on me heavily and making pained whimpers. We wobbled on, looking at clocks—for time was getting short—looking for a phone to call a cab, looking and feeling miserable and anxious, which we genuinely were.

Somehow, we reached the vicinity of the Cross with seven or eight minutes to spare, and once again I ventured a few nervous questions of passersby. The first man I approached was a retarded alcoholic who cast dumb, frosty eyes on me for a moment and then hawked a wad of phlegm at my feet. The second was "a stranger here myself, you know." The third, obviously well moistened by a few pints of red or bitter, told me we were a block off target, that we wanted the Stratford Blue, which stopped only at the Cock Horse Tavern. We checked his instructions against those of three others who passed. Two of them, like the proprietor of a dairy shop into which I desperately dashed, knew nothing at all about buses.

Three legged fashion, we hurried down to the Cock Horse. Nobody in the parking lot there, in the tavern, or in the sweet shop next door could give us assurance that we were where we should be. It was now 6:05, and I surrendered and decided to get a taxi all the way to Stratford, even though the fare and the tip run to 48s., or $6.72. The decision was not simple to act upon, for I could find no nearby phone, and I had to go hunting once more, leaving Patty standing out of the rain under an awning and looking forlornly after me as she balanced on one leg, like a stork.

I bolted into the Cromwell Arms Hotel and asked the desk clerk, an elderly woman, if there was a phone handy. "A phone, sir? Hm. Let me see. Did you try the Horse Fair: There's one there, I'm sure."

I did not reply to her as I raced out. I thought that departing quietly would be to my benefit and hers. I flew back to the Cross and found a phone booth, but I found also that the jingling freight of English coins that had been tearing at my pocket stitches with every one of the frantic strides I had so long been making did not include a "thruppence," the only coin the slot would accept. Getting one required four more inquiries, but finally I had one, was able to get through to Trinder's taxi, and, at last, to get under way to Stratford with Patty, who had limped up after me to the cab rank.

Once in the cab, I saw a small placard identifying the vehicle as "Trinder's Easy"—rather than another of its kind, "Trinder's Baker" or "Trinder's Charley," I understood, but right then I saw the ironist's mockery behind the terms.

The ride out to Stratford in the sheeting rain was close to perilous. The driver responded with manic zest to my request for a rapid trip. Schussing down the curves of Sunrising Hill was, consequently, a chancy few minutes that kept our eyelids from blinking even once until the descent was over. Our meeting with Wells and our late supper with him and Dr. Anne Righter of Cambridge were, nevertheless, thoroughly enjoyable.

Before going to the Swan for Leek soup, prawns, gammon, chips, and a carafe of vin rose, we worked and chatted and had gin and tonics in the Shakespeare Institute, in a book littered room which looked out on beautiful gardens stretching immaculately and colorfully to New Place. In the middle of the vista was an intriguing gazebo sort of thing once used by Marie Corelli when she owned the big house now used by the Institute. Her less than epic books were all about, and Dr. Wells told us that large numbers of people of a certain kind still come to Stratford because Mme. Corelli lived there, not because Shakespeare did. He is often embarrassed by their questions about her work, about which he pretends to a blissful and carefully preserved ignorance. He told us also that one dowager once consoled him, when he told her that he couldn't read much Corelli, by noting, "Yes, her books are deep."

Our return to the Abbey was a sharp contrast to our outbound journey, for Dr. Wells drove us back in his car. The ride, though thick fog had rolled over the narrow road, was a happily uneventful one.

And so was most of today. Patty and I got a good bit of work done in the Minstrel's Gallery office, posted a pack of letters, and ordered the files. Late in the afternoon we walked through the village again, primarily because Patty was hit by homesickness and wanted some change of scene to put a stop to some of the moping she found herself unable to avoid. Coming back we were caught in a downpour, but we ran under a giant old beech and by that time Patty was able to joke about the "tree adders" an ancient Wroxton visitor had told us she always prepared against by raising a parasol whenever she was near overhanging branches.

    We watched the tapering off of the rain for ten minutes or so, hurried through the last mist of it into the Abbey, and had an authoritative scotch with water before a good dinner all alone in the big dining hall. As a waiter, a waitress, and the chef himself fussed about our table, we felt regal but awkward and lonely. The royal head, I remembered in the midst of the baronial accoutrements all about me, is heavy with isolation.

    After dinner, we dropped in at the North Arms, the pub just outside the college gates. We had sherry and a long talk with a young girl from the Madison campus who attended Wroxton last spring and stayed on as an assistant in the pub's saloon bar. (She is going back home shortly, she told us.) The appealing old pub—the building, a villager told me, is about 500 years old—pleased us greatly with its blackened beams and old brasses gleaming after centuries of polishing, and we walked back up the Abbey road, at about 9:15, almost light hearted in the heavy darkness not brightened at all by a rust colored moon barely visible through the sluggish racks of the fog.

    We were making ironic jokes about the hearty cheerfulness of the Abbey. (It was illuminated only by the lamps in the servants' two fourth floor rooms and two sixty watt bulbs in the Great Hall as we climbed the front door staircase—with exaggerated caution, for the past four days' rain and the night's dank mist had given the antique and foot hollowed slate a slickness like that of fish scale.) Our pleasantries died abruptly when we found the outside door firmly bolted. We had known that our key was good only for the second door inside the vestibule, but, knowing also that the night porter's duties ran till 11:00, we had felt no worry and had seen no need to take along a key to the lower courtyard door. We should have reckoned upon the porter's apparent absent mindedness and his present anxiety about his cancer stricken wife, which led him to plan to shut up two hours early and not give us warning as we left. Our situation was wonderful.

 There we were in the dripping blackness, rattling great Jacobean doors, feeling our way up terrace steps, poking tentatively about Stygian sunken courts, and raising helpless cries for assistance from four domestics who understand only Spanish and whose privacy was protected from our noise by their sealed leaded windows, small amber squares sixty feet above us in the dark. For 15 minutes we whistled, hooped, and sang out in unison, primarily to rouse the two Joses, Isobel, or Manuel, but partly also simply to reassure ourselves.

 After a week at the Abbey we had come to terms with the resident ghosts—an elderly lady and a monk, we had been told—about which we had heard the day that we arrived, but just a few minutes before we found ourselves locked out, we had learned at the pub of two more. One of them, one of the Lord Norths, we could welcome into our spectral family matter of factly. The Earl is said merely to wander over the lawns looking straight ahead

Wroxton Abbey illuminated at night

through squinting eyes and recognizing no one, not even foreign usurpers of his grounds. The other one seemed less easy to accept. A murderer hanged in a nearby marsh for the killing of a young girl, he is, our sensationalist informants told us, well known to emit moans and scramble about the very paths and courts in which we were seeking rescuers. Our clatter kept him safely off, and it eventually brought Jose #2, mumbling and shuffling like Macbeth's porter, to our aid.

    We trudged up the sighing stairs to our bedroom, past the suits of armor in the corners of three landings—they still make us a little edgy when we come upon them in the dimness late at night—and let ourselves into our large and lofty quarters by screwing a weighty four inch key into a stubborn 18th century lock. As we did so, we heard the piercing screams of a murderer's victim in a Sherlock Holmes film that the Spaniards were following on their telly two floors up, under the pointed gables in the attic. Patty had, she found, discovered a most effective remedy for homesickness, and I had met with a few additional reminders of the special quality of our days and nights at Wroxton Abbey.

2 September 1966

I have often read and heard that the English foster order and have a reverential regard for it primarily because they are fundamentally disorderly creatures. I suspect their awareness of this carefully restrained trait has something to do with their emphasis upon the sort of punctuality that, J. Brett Langstaff said — in *Oxford-1914* (New York: Vantage Press, 1965)—his Greek tutor's butler called "the essence of politeness." Their almost incessant quest for regularity and ceaseless efforts to eliminate untidiness of manner or place are everywhere evident. Those efforts are most obvious, perhaps, in the succession of gardens which line the narrow roads leading from villages like Wroxton and Drayton to towns like Banbury.

Although close up they reveal pleasant individual touches, they seem, as they flash by a bus or car widow, almost identical. In virtually every one, the rusty ironstone earth is rich, dark, and weed free about the canes of roses luxuriantly in bloom.

Among the roses are clumps of geranium, fuschia, snapdragons, ageratum, and similarly bright plantings. All the plots seem also to be just about the same lovely little size, about fifteen or twenty feet square and walled in by privet, yew, or fencing of wood, metal, or native stone. A five or ten mile broken string of them, colorful as it may be, can become monotonous and somehow a bit depressing.

And so can several other features of the solid, dependable life the Englishman seems ever anxious to sustain. Queues form everywhere as a sort of spontaneous mass reflex. Imperatives adorn the walls of shops, restaurants, and hotels, and frown down from street signs and bus ceilings. On the Midland Red Line this morning, for example, I noted these signs: "The passenger is reminded that he must present his ticket for inspection." "Place used tickets in this slot." "Do not stand near this platform whilst the bus is in motion." "Ring the bell once only to signal the operator of the vehicle." In the storage tunnel of the Abbey I have frequently seen on the sides of used cardboard cartons the warning that "This tray will be charged at 2s. unless returned."

And the Abbey instruction booklet, prepared by the English staff here, consists of eight pages of statements reasonably well represented by these few: "Faculty and Students should not bathe in either of the Lakes...The College Authorities reserve the right to enter any room at any time for purposes of instruction... Hand in your key to the College Office...Keys not returned will be charged at 2£ each...Students must use the Garden Room Entrance to the College until 6 p.m. and after that time the Main Hall Entrance until 11 p.m...Students are reminded that all accidents, sickness or injuries, however, minor, must be reported...

Do not replace an electric bulb [most of them are 40 watt] with a more powerful one…Throwing water, snow or any other substance into, from within or towards the College buildings, is forbidden…Articles of food must be kept in glass, plastic or metal containers…Guests to meals and other resident guests must pay in advance…If you have a Radio Receiver you should obtain a license, price 25/d., from the General Post Office…"

Admittedly such regulations have a peculiar justification in this ancient house, but they seem pretty much of a piece with the rules, written and unwritten, which guide the natives outside these walls. It all seems part of the system which multiplies the gardens; dictates a potted plant in back of a thousand windows in succession; and makes an instant reflex of "Sorry," "`kyou," and "Please." The same impulse produces little name placards over the doorways of shabby row houses identified as "Ivydene" or "Close Cottage" in imitation of the namings of the grander holdings and estates on the fringes of towns.

One sees the system at work in the supermarkets, where each customer does his own bagging of his purchases. He sees it in first class railway cars in which passenger after passenger will back off from a "Reserved" card on a seat which has already been empty for half an hour and obviously will not be claimed by its purchaser.

Like the gardens, these other evidences of some prevalent power supported by an almost universal solicitude for it can, I think, charm an American and make him feel envious, but they can also make him strangely melancholy and full of longing for the scrap and scuffle, the variegated confusion, even the reassuring—if shocking—wastefulness of his land's ways. He feels something like hunger, for instance, for big, strong Kraft paper bags instead of the flimsy ones he must bear so responsibly here, for books of matches scattered freely about (one pays 3d. for one of them to an English tobacconist) for free delivery service, for 3 hour dry-cleaning facilities catering to his procrastination and slipshod wardrobe habits.

He also finds himself longing for American slickness of decor, even if plasticized, in places of business as he views the 1930-ish appointments of a provincial English bank, the tawdry and tasteless jumble of clashing designs and colors in a Banbury fabric shop, the rummage sale disorder of an ironmonger's. And as he does so, he is reminded that the "the system" is not so all-pervading as it might seem, that he really has no right at all for thinking of the English as hive bound and wondering how in God's name they make love to each other or write wild and wonderful literature.

He remembers the other half of the game that the system really is, the abandoned and crazy part of it. This part permits the fearfully sound, over disciplined, and frostily sensible Englishman to carry about coins which will buy nothing at all, to quote prices in a unit of currency that does not exist, to elect twice as many MPs as can be seated at any one time, and to cling stubbornly to currency arrangements and driving habits seen as quaintly perverse by most of the rest of the world.

3 September 1966

*[I devoted this day of journal-writing to composing the
following letter to a friend back home:]*

Patty and I have just finished reading your letter as we breakfasted. Your news of home brightened our meal, a typical Wroxton one in that the bacon was strikingly like what I imagine uncooked ear lobe would be and the fried eggs featured yolks the consistency of Turkish taffy and whites floating in oleaginous puddles. (The fats and greases here are poured out in Brobdingnagian fashion by the chef, and regular items like squooshy chips and fried bread and fish are doing astounding things to our visceras, which mutter and percolate busily whenever we deny them their generous daily allotments of entero-vioform.)

    Our cheerfulness and contentment as we read were enriched by a feeling of righteousness, for we knew that we were receiving your message at an hour when you were either just returning from some Spanish debauch or lying slugabed. We thank you for your note and hope that we can expect another sometime soon.

We are still, of course, getting used to the Abbey, our job, the village, Banbury, and the English and their ways. We are in our permanent quarters in Room 2, now, after five days or so in Room 1 while the Haberlys were here. Digs here, as you know, are handsome but a piece of real estate rather than a bed and bath. The bedroom, I would say, is nearly 40x25, the bath about 10x18. The ceiling, richly figured with strapwork and gilded pendants, hovers some sixteen feet above us. The north wall, on the left of the Abbey, is given over almost wholly to the eight-light casement window through which I can right now see a sloping green bank heavily wooded with beeches, oaks, and evergreens like the towering and aged yew near the "croquey" green.

Patty and I never get in each other's way, not even when we fly into sudden constitutional jogs, but we do feel a peculiar kind of isolation, especially whenever we find ourselves a little smarmy about Madison. We have also had some difficulty in adjusting to Jacobean carvings in The Necessary, in which, as I have hinted, we have been spending more than a decent share of our time. Hour by hour, however, the mini-flat is becoming home to us, as are all the roughly sixty rooms of this giant old place.

The Davises—Ricky and his constantly snitty wife who serve jointly as business managers here—are, as I told Chris Hewitt [English Department chair in 1966] in a letter of which he may have spoken to you, are less easy to come to terms with. They are still attempting the Mrs. Jewkes or Mrs. Danvers technique with me, but the lordly manner that I have affected as I stride about, tweed jacketed, crisply capped, and slapping vigorously at imaginary riding boots with an imaginary baton, has, I think, given them pause in their formerly obvious resolve to pin me to some rustling garret cot while a sodden and lustful neighboring barley farmer has his way with me. My memos, masterpieces, if I say so myself, of taut organization, self-sufficiency, Latinate terms, and a few obscure literary allusions, seem to have likewise helped serve my purposes, and I doubt that I shall have any real trouble with "Ricky" or "Linnie."

    About my work, itself, I am much less sanguine. After only a week of use, my desk calendar is a palimpsest of scribbles which, I hope, will remind me at the proper times to do things like (1) tell the chef that Miss Remas is allergic to fish and tell the college physician that two other women must never be given penicillin or sulfa; (2) invite Messrs. Gibbard and Portergill to dinner to discuss a Banbury Rotary project for our students; (3) arrange a tea or sherry for the Reverend W.J. Smart from Sulgrave Vicarage, where I am soon to join some Americans like our Ambassador and an Air Force high muckety-muck at an Anglo-American vesper service—covered by B.B.C.—in honor of Washington's family; (4) contact the Hamilton Galleries in London about a Wroxton hanging of the paintings of an American artist, Ann Cole Philips; (5) make a text-buying excursion to Blackwell's in Oxford; (6) meet an Oxford official about lecturers' dates; (7) confirm a series of field-trip reservations dates for the "Friendly Midland Red" Motor Bus Co.; and (8) write, phone, and visit about two dozen academics, professional men, and public officials whom I may be able to secure as lecturers or tutors.

Lesser matters, like the fact that, as of now, Rutherford [FDU central administration] has not, in spite of my letters and cables, put a penny in the Wroxton till at Barclay's Bank and that academic preparations for the semester are being financed by my personal traveler's checks, are daily stuffed into various don't-forget niches of my mind. (Several of our academic devices here make inevitable a kind of giggling chaos. If, for instance, a lutanist, a member of Parliament, or an expert on 13th-century tiles happens to get sick, sozzled, or stubborn, the delicately balanced schedule for a forthcoming week or two must be hastily revised. Existing reservations for buses must be canceled and new ones set. The chef must be warned that we will, after all, be home for lunch and dinner on Tuesday, not mousing around Oxford or Stratford or Bath. And all conferences and review and assignment sessions with students have to be moved to new slots.

Dealing with such contingencies might rather easily produce in me the nystagmus about which I have my little phobia, but it can also be exciting and full of lovely, small quietnesses. Two examples of what I have in mind are these: (1) Mrs. Scott, who runs the miniature grocery store in the village, has rapidly acceded to my request that she add a few items to her stock—ruled note paper, some kind of tobacco besides "Digger," a black and vile plug of formidable power, and oddments like scotch tape and pen refills. "Whatever you want, sir, you just tinkle. Mr. Scott's a dead hand at getting things in." (2) Because Dean H. has found that Blackwell's is hopelessly sluggish about filling book orders, we do much of our text buying at the Banbury Children's Book Shop. I stood in it the other day, fussed over by the matronly owner and her solicitous young clerk, and wrote out orders for the O.E.D.

and a history text as I ducked my head under a "Beatrix Potter Centenary" banner. I do not expect to be bored by my duties.

The people here are also endlessly fascinating studies for an American, or at least for me, new and naive as I am in this clime. I entertained two Banbury officials the other evening, a farmer and a real estate man. For two hours they chatted with me, not only about the business we had to discuss, but about fox hunting, Switzerland, France, Spain, and Italy, which they have recently visited, the carvings in the Abbey Chapel ("Not met often, is it, that bit—the fifth panel showing the circumcision of Christ?"), and the eleven Earls of Guilford who ruled this manor. They also told me that the big evergreens here are not, as I assumed, sequoias, but Wellingtonias, and that the Banbury history book I was reading was less good than three others I could get.

Today the relief cook here gave me a ride into Banbury and back. As his dilapidated midget Reliant rattled down the narrow road on the three wheels over which it is triangularly balanced, he rattled on about the Mediterranean countries he had been to last year, about birds—he had seen a kestrel swoop across our route—and about English justice. ("Shockin', it is, the way they'll savage you for petty things.") As we pulled out of the parking lot in which he had left his car for ten minutes, he braked to a halt, vaulted out the door, and raced over to a white-smocked attendant snoozing a block away in the sun. When he got back into the car, he apologized to me: "Forgot the sixpence charge, I did. 'Tisn't my way to go off without paying."

These sorts of experiences suggest pretty well my reasons for regarding the English with admiration, affection, and occasional envy. Their sense of order, their good manners, their good talk, their intellectual curiosity and range of interests have been remarkably pleasant surprises to me, even though you had given me advance notice of them. Conversations and books, as well, had theoretically prepared me for their eccentricity, or at least singularity, but even so, the concrete examples of it that I have met have left me blinking.

The sewer-line excavations here brought a number of "oners" on the run. Elderly architects, young students, infirm widows, and brisk fellows with hearty mutton-chop tufts have been crawling in and out of the ditch. Amateurs all, they have nevertheless been professionally precise in their sifting of clay for bits of tile or stained glass or building blocks. They have taken color slides of the fragments, have measured the gleanings and the depth of the strata in which they were found, and used magnifying glasses to study the direction of the chisel marks on the stones once part of a 13th-century church wall.

Some of them came to pursue two or three interests at once. One country-gentry-lady type, about sixty, frequently interrupted her study of the dig with dashes to some thicket to spot a yellowhammer, a Spanish owl, or one of the barking deer lately observed in the vicinity. Others, like a thin and angular granny with an immobile face, were memorable for attributes that had nothing to do with historical or archaeological keenness. She carried an umbrella on a sunny afternoon because she had heard that tree adders, a threat, I gather, only to her, frequently fling themselves like arrows from branches at victims strolling beneath the trees.

Not all things English, of course, have me entranced. Some of the English ways, in fact have mildly and, in one or two instances, even heavily depressed me. The order—in the inevitable garden plots, the putting-green lawns, and queues which form, apparently whenever any pedestrian stops for a moment anywhere—quickly becomes strangely monotonous. Interior design, in banks and clothing shops, for instance, seems to me disquietingly 1930-ish, as does the fare on the workingman's rented telly. The look of a Banbury fabric-shop window crammed full of hopeless patternings and color combinations, is, well, appalling. Paying 3d. for matches to light cigarettes three times more expensive than those in the States, bagging your own groceries in a supermarket—in a bag you are expected to have brought with you, waiting a week for pants pressing, and finding most services in provincial hotels and elsewhere suspended at 11:00 p.m. can sometimes leave you feeling slightly different than formerly about the multiplied coddling of self-indulgence back home.

If the regulations issued by the English staff of the Abbey are representative of generally prevailing attitudes, the abundance of blunt imperatives and injunctions is something else that might get to you. Here are some fair samplings of the 8-page folder: "Faculty and Students should not bathe in either of the lakes... The College Authorities [note the capital letters] reserve the right to enter any room at any time for purposes of inspection... Hand in your key to the College office...Keys not returned will be charged at £2 each...Students must use the Garden Room Entrance to the College until 6:00 p.m. and after that time the Main Hall Entrance until 11:00 p.m....Students are reminded that all accidents, sickness or injuries, however minor, must be reported...Do not replace an electric light bulb [40 w. is standard] with a more powerful one...Throwing water, snow or any other substance into, from within or towards the College buildings, is forbidden…Articles of food must be kept in glass, plastic or metal containers…Guests to meals and other resident guests must pay in advance…If you have a Radio Receiver you should obtain a license, price 25/d…If you leave your bicycle for any purpose [they are rented from the College], take the lamps and inflator with you…"

My most destructive experience, however, has been my visit yesterday to an English barber shop. The U.S. Customs booklets should include clear warnings about the danger of such foreign adventuring. It is physically and psychologically excruciating and produces marrings which, unquestionably, are irremediable. I looked in the rear-view mirror when I wakened from the anesthesia with which the surgery had been attended and promptly blacked out again. I have been trying, ever since I was brought home to convalesce, to decide just what style of "do" I received. The young sheep-shearer who had at me assured me that he would give me an "American cut," but the term would suit only if, as I now believe, he was speaking out of a violent prejudice against my native land. "Olivier's Henry V" or "The Borstal Boy" appears to me a more accurately applicable designation. I have seen only one haircut like it in my life. That one was on the head of Bruce Cabot when he portrayed a villainous Iroquois in *Last of the Mohicans* years and years ago. His appearance, a cinema shocker in its day, led, I think, to the founding of the Hays office and quick passage of the Sullivan Act. The shop in which I was actionably assaulted was named "Christo's," pronounced just like the first part of "Christopher." For me, though, the i will henceforth and ever after be long, and the t will be separated by a hyphen from the o, followed by a bold exclamation mark. I had Patty take a "close-up" photograph of the back of my head while it was still smoking hot from the drawer's knife. You shall have a good view of it, I hope, when we get home and start settling some old scores with our showings of slides.

The barber's totally unprovoked attack upon me has burdened me with a temporarily dyspeptic view of all things British, and I have been trying conscientiously all day to sweeten my contemplation of them. *The Guardian* which I have just been reading helps a good bit, particularly with its out-of-the-way columns. The personals remind me that, my barber not withstanding, the English are a people full of a tender and lasting sentiment: "In Memoriam: Everitt, William Needham, M.C. Captain 1/4th Battalion, Duke of Wellington's Regiment. Eldest son of the late Mr. and Mrs. C.K. Everitt, of Sheffield. Killed in action…on 3rd September 1916, and who has no known grave but the soil of France. In honor of his name and also of all his gallant comrades of the 1/4th and 1/5th…" In addition they provide evidence that what may seem pure maliciousness to me now may really be enigmatic playfulness: "Gemma: Wishes for a happier Navy blue anniversary. Snooker still loves the little Bocky. T.C. Ox."

This dreadfully long letter to you has been one more bit of therapy for me. Sitting so long over it, however, has begun to aggravate my old condition. I hope that it has not been too abrasive to your contact lenses. If you will promise to write us again, I will promise not to be so rankly prompt or lengthy in replying hereafter.

Note: The following sign, which I saw in at Christ Church, Oxford, leads me to believe that Mr. Davis's regulations here are by no means an indication of local eccentricity:

Christ Church Meadow

The meadow keepers and Constables are hereby instructed to prevent the entrance into the meadow of all beggars, all persons in ragged or very dirty clothes, persons of improper character or who are not decent in appearance and behaviour; and to prevent indecent, rude or disorderly conduct of every description.

- To allow no handcarts, wheelbarrows, no hawkers or persons carrying parcels or bundles so as to obstruct the walks.

- To prevent the flying of kites, throwing stones, throwing balls, bowling hoops, shooting arrows, firing guns or pistols or playing games attended with danger or inconvenience to passers by, also fishing in the waters, catching birds, bird nesting or cycling.

- To prevent all persons cutting names on, breaking or injuring the seats, shrubs, plants, trees, or turf.
- To prevent the fastening of boats or rafts to the iron palisading or river wall, and to prevent encroachments of every kind by the riverside.

THE GATES WILL CLOSE AT 9.0

4 September 1966

Patty and I had a wonderful visit by John Fritz, of the history department at Madison. He was here to talk with me about a special course which may be arranged for the Madison campus. Its title will be something like "British Antecedents of American Culture." It would begin with lectures here at Wroxton, to be conducted, we now are thinking, by Graham Webster of Birmingham University. In addition to the lectures, the students would get actual field work in archaeology at some place like Sulgrave Manor.

Our business over, he and I joined Patty for drinks in the Faculty Lounge.

Each of us had a Dewars and water there—with ice cubes to show John how much Patty and I appreciated his stopping by—and we carried our drinks with us during a tour of the Abbey and the grounds. Although we have had rain for some part of every

The thatched-roof dwellings of Wroxton Village, with the duck pond to the left

Pond on the Abbey grounds

day for a week, yesterday's late afternoon was a fine one, and we sipped our drinks and chatted and strolled, the tinkling of our ice cubes providing a pleasant little music for us. Just before we went into dinner, we sat on the moss clumped terrace wall to the east of the Abbey—the moss has tiny spikes of red capped flowers now—and laughed about the way that I had greeted John by the Duck Pond off Main Street across from the College gate. (I had flagged him down while he was still picking his way in his rented Vauxhall and told him I had come out to greet him for several reasons: I had porter's duty on Saturdays, was shying kestrels away from our wood pigeons, was checking on the growth of fairy rings, and did not want him to lose a second's opportunity to study appreciatively the handiwork of the first English barber I had visited on Thursday.)

We had a quiet good time at our joking, and I suppose that all of us years from now will find those contented moments coming back to us with a sweet sort of melancholy full of the lovely and yet softly sad colors of the sky above the Abbey's great gables, gray purples and pinks faintly gilded. I am sure that I will.

The three of us and Miss Hogan, the sprightly and charming Irish housekeeper, who is, unfortunately, leaving us shortly, had a bad dinner in the big dining hall. The relief cook, to whom I had spoken earlier in the day about John's visit, interpreted my request for a good meal as meaning a big one. He gave us five kinds of meat in a Devonshire Grill (veal cutlet, bacon rolls with something mysterious in their soft coils, sausage, hamburgers, and beefsteak), all of them a drip with cooking fat. We also had two kinds of potatoes (chips and duchess), and the omnipresent Brussels sprouts. John was gallant about the meal, or perhaps he had been rendered broadly tolerant by the third whisky I had poured for him, and even said that he enjoyed it. Patty and I, however, had our usual postprandial Wroxton pains, alarums, and excursions, and I was in our spacious bath room at 3:00 a.m., belching marvelously, swallowing at gaggings, and keeping one hand on the toilet lid and the other busy tossing milk of magnesia tablets between my teeth. From the bedroom I could hear Patty laughing sympathetically, not derisively. I have concluded that the brutality of England's barbers is exceeded only by that of its cooks.*

After dinner the three of us went to the North Arms, where we had one or two sherries and a long talk with an English family, a man, his wife, and their seventeen-year-old daughter. Our conversation was most cheerful and congenial. One result of it was that the gentleman whose name we still do not know, promised that he would come to the Abbey soon to bring a peculiar little memento of our enjoyable hour together: a clay pipe used by 17th century gravediggers, he told us, as a disinfectant after they had buried a victim of the plague. Something like 4,000 people died in the little village where he now lives, and many of them, apparently, were buried on the 14 acres which he once farmed. The first time that he plowed his ground, he said, he found thousands of the pipes in the furrows, testimony to the mythology so often passing as medical science. The superstitious

---

My several complaints about the food service in the Abbey in its earliest years are, happily, not representative of the fare served later on, when the College employed its own kitchen staff in place of the catering group on hand in the first few years of the college's existence.

corpse bearers believed that if they took three or four puffs of tobacco after handling each of the victims and then threw away the pipe, they would ward off infection.

Patty and I look forward to getting this curiosity. We hope, too, that we can look forward to more heartening visits like John Fritz's. Both of us were full of regret when he drove off early this morning, headed for home as we headed for an almost wholly deserted Abbey, dreary under gray skies and a light rain.

10 September 1966

The following letter to the editor appeared this morning in either *The Times or The Telegraph*, I forget which, under the heading, "'Runaway Engine": "Sir It is reported in your columns (Sept. 6) that a locomotive, by its own volition, ran away from Carnforth, and was not overtaken for nine miles.

I have it on record that in October, 1859, an almost exactly similar incident took place on the London, Brighton, & South Coast Railway, when early one morning a locomotive (unattended) gently puffed its way out of the shed at Petworth, and was not arrested until a courageous railways servant swung himself on to the footplate and shut off the regulator.

Is it not time that British Railways learned the lesson? Yours faithfully, A.C. Johnstone. Ruislip, Middx."

The English, I keep reminding myself with good reason, are not a simple people. On the one hand, they fuss and bluster in their pubs, parlors, and papers about issues that must seem quaint to strangers among them like me. Long before I came here, I followed a rather extended exchange of *Guardian* letters about the night jar's call and about the proper way to idle. And just about a week ago I heard the local vicar say that he was going to have to get "a bit shirty" soon about the commercialization of his Wroxton parish, in which the opening of a tiny gift shop has increased the business enterprises by 33 1/3% (A pub and a village grocery were all that was here previously.)

Like Americans and all other people, they also rail constantly at their government and all in its purview. In the three weeks or so that I have been here, I haven't heard a good word for Wilson or Labour. Most of my academic correspondents have been instantly testy about the "imbecile" currency regulations. Bank clerks, cab drivers, shop girls, gardeners, and roof thatchers have indignantly spoken to me of the medical services program, the wage price freeze, the Rhodesian policy, the non-decimal money system, the dole, the immigration rules—applying especially to Pakistanis and Jamaicans who "come to squat here for public assistance, the dirty trots"—and the English workman's laziness. ("Top doss labour is seldom seen. Most of the blokes just tickle around.")

And yet, in many respects they have a capacity for bearing discomfort, distress, even disaster, so quietly that an unsympathetic observer might characterize them as marked by a bovine hebetude. The gentry can engage in sprightly, graceful conversation over sherry and biscuits and create an air of genuine elegance even though their tweeds may be roughly worn and stained, their cigarette pack may have only two or three carefully husbanded survivors in it, and the gathering for which one of their number has paid may have forced him to effect prudent economies in some department of his household budget.

Two stories I've recently heard comment unflatteringly on one set of the paradoxical attributes of these complicated people. The first, obviously Gallic in origin and indecent as well as unkind, runs this way: A Frenchman, strolling along a beach came upon a friend having his way with a distinctly unresponsive woman. "Pierre! Pierre!" he cried. "Arretez vous! That woman, she is dead!" "Mon dieu!" Pierre replied, "I thought she was English." The other more fairly represents what I judge to be the proper perspective. It deals with two Englishwomen who were lamenting their sexual obligations to their mates. "But, my dear," sighed one, "it is so awful! How do you stand it?" "Oh," the second answered, "I just grit my teeth and think of England."

Perhaps it is this teeth gritting love of homeland that explains much about them. I came upon my first instance of it twenty three years ago—almost to the the day—in Italy, when I was wounded along with more than a dozen others knocked down by one mortar shell. The casualty nearest me was Clar Wyld, of Glossop, Derbyshire. He was hit worse than I and bled profusely from several non-fatal but serious wounds in the head, face, and chest. During our four mile trip to the evac hospital he groaned frequently with pain and worried two or three times about the blood that had filled his eyes. He did some suffering, I know, for several hours on his hospital cot next to mine.

Just before dark, a crisp sister gave all of us a very strong cup of tea. Clar, whose face bandages had by that time been pushed up over his brows, raised up weakly and drank his, with tentative sippings at first and then in tongue scalding gulps. Within ten minutes, he was up from his cot. "I'm off to the half track," he whispered to me as he crept out. "Like a silly ass I left the code book by the radio. It won't do to leave that lying around for Jerry. I'll be back." In about an hour and a half he was back, with his code book and a happy report that getting rides both ways was easy. I don't think he was able to get on his feet again until more than a week later.

Every day here I witness Englishmen performing in a manner really quite similar to—if under circumstances less critical than—Clar's. I have had a ride to town with a man whose cheerfulness was not at all dampened by the fact that his car's second gear failed frequently or that one of the doors was secured by a stout rope. I have heard the daughter-in-law of Lady Pearson (who occupied the Abbey as a tenant before FDU bought it) fondly recollect that her mother-in-law, when she leased the Abbey, resolutely wrapped an afghan about her seventy some year old ankles and greeted with quick impatience all complaints about the drafty old mansion's frostiness.

Yesterday on the Banbury Tysoe bus with Patty, I rose to give my seat to a heavily burdened woman in her forties. "Not a bit of it, duck," she smiled. "This is jolly good here." As a return for my gallantry she did agree that I should put one of her several large parcels between my feet. As we drove along I looked out at Banburians standing meditatively or chattily in twisting queues inside post office and cleaning shop doors or musing through the windscreens of their little cars caught in one of the traffic snarls made unending by the narrow main streets and highways.

Patty and I got off the bus with Jessie Cook, the woman who opens her living room as the village post office and who had been marketing in Banbury. Jessie walked briskly because the time was 4:40, and her second postal time block should begin each weekday at 4:30. When the three of us reached her cottage we came upon three villagers who had arrived promptly at 4:30 to buy stamps. They were busily expressing concern about the "wretched little blue tits," chickadee-like birds here which have learned to spot the milkman's rounds and to tear holes in the aluminum foil caps of delivered pintas so that they can sip off a quarter inch or so of cream. "Nasty little things," one woman was clucking. "Let the wasps into the bottles, they do." They greeted Jessie warmly. None of them showed the least impatience about her being fifteen minutes late.

 Something more than a species of spiritual regard for tooth gritting may, however, be involved in the production of their sturdy quality. The services and products available may have a large part in shaping the character of those for whom they exist. One or two of my notes earlier in this journal serve as partial examples of what I have in mind. My sampling of "TCP," one of the few English mouthwashes I have seen on Banbury's shelves, can be cited as another evidence. It's nauseating, a curious blending of creosote and formaldehyde. Its remarkable taste lingers for hours, even when one dilutes the liquid with five parts of water and has a hearty breakfast right after using it. I read the label last evening as I flapped my still beefy tongue about in my mouth and noted that Englishmen are advised to swish the substance around twice daily.

 I thought of their toilet paper, their barbers, their cooks, and their market places' open air fish stalls in which a side of plaice may lie, unrefrigerated—in the sun and under attack by flies and wasps—for eight hours or more. My reflections helped me to accept a little less incredulously the conduct of the Clar Wylds. They also, I admit with a touch of regret, diminished ever so slightly my previously boundless awe and admiration over this people's indestructible thumbs up defiance to the worst of Hitler's fire bombings.

Top and Bottom: Wroxton students in the 1967 Stratford Shakespeare's birthday parade

5 November 1966

A good bit of the program is honestly remarkable. The good points plentiful. Yesterday, for instance, we heard an M.P. full of elegance and practical political wisdom, and this coming Thursday we are meeting him in London for another talk and a guided tour of Parliament. Just a little while ago we had a brilliant lecture by Inga Stina Ewbank, a Swedish scholar from the University of Liverpool, who cast her prepared notes aside and fashioned a marvelous impromptu analysis of Tourneur's *Revenger's Tragedy*, just a week before all of us were to see it at Stratford. (The production is the first major one in about 300 years, and it is reportedly really fine. Ted Ross [English department faculty member] had run up from his London sabbatical digs to see it, and he and I and Rhoda and Patty literally bumped into each other in the lobby.)

Wroxton students 1966–1967

Students in costume, from left to right: Diane Guidera, Rudy Thoren, Susan Siegel, Thomas Shanklin

We've been to castles, universities, schools, village meetings, shrines, cathedrals, and landmarks of all sorts and have been visited by some of Britain's best scholars and lecturers. (One of them even came from Edinburgh to meet our classes.) We've heard, in addition, directors, actors, musicians, architects, political organizers, mayors, solicitors, museum keepers, and amateur and professional archaeologists. One of our lectures we heard in the 14th-century schoolroom where Shakespeare studied as a boy and four more in the Institute where a team of Shakespeareans is now preparing a new edition of the plays. The first of our "Schools and Schooling" lectures was presented by an Eton master in the High Room where several prime ministers had their early lessons. Another, on British prehistory, will soon be offered in the Ashmolean Museum by the Senior Keeper.

As a result of some letters I wrote to the Banbury Historical Society and a local industrialist, two of our students, working respectively on 17th-century puritanism and marketing techniques, are drawing upon a unique ms. of sermons by a 1600 Banbury preacher named Whately and data made available by a local coffee-making subsidiary of General Foods. Still another student, having visited Stratford seven times and read Jan Kott and Martin Esslin, is analyzing the R.S.C.'s absurdist modifications of Shakespeare's plays.

All of this is cause for delight, and on at least three days of every week here I am convinced that I am in a kind of academic Elysium.

4 December 1966

A long time has passed since my last entry, I notice. Well, I have been busy. I think I recently told someone back home that I have been spending most of my days here struggling up a greased pole mounted in a nest of adders and that right now I am climbing like hell to stay even. The figure seems apt, if undistinguished. Day after day, week after week, I have been contending with the scheduling problems here. Will Dr. Bulpitt call me tomorrow to confirm his coming for a lecture six days hence? Does Mr. Madagan's failure to respond—for more than ten days—to my letter mean that he will not come to lecture twice this coming Tuesday, or that he has somehow forgotten the appointment? When I reschedule the appearance of Brian Davison (who misunderstood the timing for his visit which I telephoned him about in London), I must remember to call Blinkhorn's: the slide projector, hired for Davison's first canceled lecture, must be reserved for the make up date.

What about the next all day coach trip? Have I, or has Patty, checked to make sure that Blenheim Palace or Warwick Castle will be open at the hour at which our group arrives? And where is the confirmation letter from Midland Red Omnibus Co.? Has something happened to the letter I sent a week ago to Mr. Sparkes in Traffic? (Further note for tickler file on this trip: Ask

Walter and Patty Savage enjoying a formal dinner at the Abbey

chef either to stop featuring lettuce and butter sandwiches in the box lunches or, if those bland things are a sine qua non, to wrap them in foil rather than napkins so that the lettuce does not turn brown during its overnight and following morning wait in the lunch boxes. And tell him definitely no more pork pies, for which the students seem to hold me personally responsible.)

I must remember, too, to get someone on the crew here to readjust the radiators in the Library Lecture Hall. One of them creates a sirocco on one side of the room, and the other one is a rather infuriatingly ironic ornament amidst the frigidity which surrounds it.

Thus goes the train of events associated with getting someone behind the lectern as often as possible for our class meetings. The processes are often full of anxiety. Our deadline for printing a week's schedule of lectures quizzes, trips, and the like is early afternoon of the preceding Friday. More than once I have received acceptances from tentatively listed lecturers as late as 1:00 p.m. on the deadline day. On four different occasions, listed faculty have failed to appear. In each instance their reasons for withdrawing have been good ones—sickness, a sudden summons to duties elsewhere—but their need to withdraw has been explained to me at the eleventh hour, and their inability to come has required either a rearranging of the week's program or a somewhat jerry built carrying on with it in its diminished proportions.

By and large, though, supervising the strictly academic details of Wroxton days has been a duty full of rich and rare rewards, intellectually and socially. Patty and I have spent happy and stimulating hours in the company of dozens of people who have, indirectly or directly, been associated with the conduct of the courses or the Abbey. With remarkably few exceptions, our guests and hosts have been delightful companions.

1985

28 January 1985

Starting this entry late this evening, I recalled other similarly incongruous yokings in my experience of the day. On a walk around the Abbey grounds in the morning, after breakfast at the hotel, I'd seen a moorhen, belly down, its wings spread in a gesture of flight frozen in the ice still on Lady Lake. A few yards further on, I saw beech saplings 2 or 3 inches in diameter supported by four inch thick stakes cut from dead trees just as, on the train from London, I had seen saplings staked in the same way in an old graveyard. Many of the tombstones had toppled, others were tilting, but the saplings braced by deadwood were growing, at intervals as carefully and regularly measured as the grave plots themselves. A minute's walk further on, I saw a dead blue tit bent double at the base of a soaring lime tree. Its glazing eyes looked sightlessly up toward the topmost branches. Fifty yards past that spot, I saw the Great Pond. Half of it, the shadier west end, I think, was a dull pewter color under ice. The other end, warmed by sun, was an olive mirror reflecting tree trunks, reeds, sky.

Finally, I recalled Robert Denton, our groundsman, and Jessie Cook, for 40 years in charge of Wroxton's post office, to which I had gone in mid afternoon to buy a Cadbury bar from the small candy shelf.

Mrs. Cook sat behind the counter, hunched over and peering at postal-savings forms. As I entered she squinted against the pale light filtering, through a window near which I stood, into the tiny, shadowy room. "Why it's Professor Savage," she exclaimed softly in some surprise. "I don't know why it was," she went on, "but I was thinking about you just the other day." There was no further reference to the fact that we had not met for over six years, but I suspected that she intended the seemingly casual comment as a grateful recognition of my return to the village—and of the return in her reminiscence of the older village days of which my appearance reminded her.

With no fear of any egotistical overemphasis on my importance, I believe that my turning up again pleased her greatly. Yet her manner hardly changed, just as it had not changed twenty years before when she told me of the death of a beloved neighbor. I am willing to believe that, privately, Mrs. Cook has her passions and dreams, secret rages and covert desperations. Publicly, however, she maintains in moments of emergency, joy, and grief, the same demeanor of calm and mild astonishment with which I have heard her discuss the raids of blue tits or wasps upon the puncturable caps of the pint bottles left on her porch by the milkman: "The wretched little beggars have been at it again. The birds make the holes, they do, and the wasps squeeze in. Devilish milk nickers, they are, the lot of them."

 I had encountered Robert for the first time again during one of my walks around the lake. "Hello," he called out with a hint of a smile and immediately directed my attention to the poor condition of the "Christmas trees" planted among the much taller, much faster growing poplars. The poplars love the wetness of the particular boggy area we were in, he informed me, much more than the beeches and Norway spruce do.

 A note of intense indignation sharpened his tone as he continued his characterization of poplars. (They are full of water. He has an instrument that measures water content of trees, and the poplar's is the highest. They are not much good for anything. They are not nearly as "griceful" as the beech. The wood is too soft for lumber, and they crowd out better trees.) He especially dislikes one species of poplar, to which he refers as an "almbow," or something similar.

 He paused in his disquisition on trees to pick up his pitchfork and push and stir up the fire he had built to burn up the pile created by his clearing and pruning. I asked him if the droppings I had seen on the slope above the wooded plot in which we stood were signs of the munt jac deer that I was eagerly trying to get a look at. "No, rabbits, I should think. Come along here. I shall show you some deer pellets. They're long and thin, is deer pellets." He searched about in the carpet of wet leaves, swinging a heavy muddy boot left and right ahead of him as he moved along. "No. I must have disturbed them in the tidying up today. I saw them yesterday. That's cornus, there," he said, stooping to pick up a small branch waiting for the fire. "Dogwood. You have that in the States, don't you? Grows wild all over here, but the garden centers charge you one pound fifty for a potted plant this size."

I asked him about a fairly large burrowing hole I had seen near the Great Pond on my walk. "That'd be a rabbit. It could be a fox, but I should think a rabbit there. Here's one over here by this great old poplar stump." He pointed out the hole and then called my attention to a large wound on a nearby beech. "The rabbit did that," he said, shaking his head in dismay. "The rabbits, the deer, and the squirrels all damage the gardens and trees. John Seagrave has a slide of a beech sapling a squirrel barked in one day, the whole tree top to bottom. It's a masters the damage they can do. The whole tree stripped bare. I've never seen the like. The squirrel that did it didn't get away free. I shot it, I did. The people in the forestry service have to shoot some of the deer. They'd lose their trees, else. We have just two pair of deer here, so I don't trouble them."

We finished our talk and I left him whistling and thrashing at the clippings, not seeing him again till well after 5:00. Clad in garments the color of the earth and woodlands, he was driving a bright yellow tractor up the black-topped Abbey main road toward the village. As he drove, he cocked an ear at the racket of rooks in an oak he rumbled under. I watched him and recalled three earlier experiences with him.

The first was in 1966, when he was a young assistant to the Scot who was then head gardener. I called his attention to a holly tree near the walk in front of the Abbey, telling him that one of the branches was growing right out into the path. Did he think it should be cut back? He didn't. He was definite about that. "Ivery toim I koot it, soombody in the village doys."

The second was in the spring of 1967, when he was about 18 or 19 and I was about to board a coach in which I was taking a large party of undergraduates to Coventry. "Where are you goin', then, today, guvnor?" he asked. I told him, and he said, "Ah, Coventry. A smashing place, I hear. I should like to see it one day," he sighed, suggesting that it was a jet flight away.

For more than fifty years the gardens of Wroxton Abbey have been lovingly maintained by members of the Denton family

The last occurrence was in June, 1984, when I talked with him about some trouble he was having with his kidneys. He was all right, he assured me, while he was in Wroxton. It was when he got to Banbury that he felt pain. "It's the hard paving underfoot," he said. "Here, on the sward I have no trouble at all."

Just before he turned the tractor leftward toward the gate house at the meeting of virtually all of Wroxton's streets—Church Street, Mills Lane, Main Street, Dark Lane—Robert turned and saw me on the path, under the oriel window. He stopped the tractor, climbed down, and hurried toward me. "I got the picture you left for me last year," he said, referring to an engraving of the Abbey. "It looks foin on the wall. Iverybody as cooms in comments on it. I've been wantin' to thank you."

He was clearly embarrassed, had probably been thinking throughout the day of the proper form for these remarks of gratitude. "You're welcome, Robert," I replied quickly. "I like it too, but I like the walking stick you carved for me much better." His whole body relaxed and a smile softened his face. "Do you use it, then? I'm glad of that." And he walked back to his tractor with which he breaks the earth of which he himself seems in part compounded, mounted it, and drove away, in the direction of his Wroxton House flat and his wife, an American from Buffalo.

Now, late at night as I write these lines, I sit here thinking about the relationship between the singer and the song. Who am I to encapsulate someone like Peter or the hotel girl or Robert Denton in sentences passing judgment, favorable or unfavorable? Whether or not I have said what I've said well or badly, whether or not my judgments are valid or invalid isn't the point. What is important is that I did the saying, the judging. I issued the pronouncements, admitted or excluded evidence and handed down verdicts. I, who felt inexplicable cold drafts upon the back of my neck as I bent over my tablet in the little pool of rusty yellow light in the dark of the vast old bedroom—the neck of someone not really the writer of these lines, I concluded, and shivered just a little.

11 February 1985

The events of the last few days convince me that we have poltergeists, if not ghosts, with us in the Abbey. Their mischievous misconduct is a reassuring scapegoating explanation of the mishaps, small emergencies, and obstacles that have almost continuously frustrated our recent progress. Friday's five inch snowfall, accompanied by drift producing winds and frigid temperatures that turned roadways into stretches of glare ice, forced the indefinite postponement of Saturday's Oxford tour. The storm also kept some of our suppliers, much of our service staff, and, today, one of our lecturers from getting to the Abbey.

One of our two furnaces has been operating unreliably and causing all of us and our hot water taps to run cold. The exercise room equipment that was supposed to have been delivered Friday or today is still not here. One of the three washing machines is malfunctioning. The chef's refrigerator is out of order. Three of

Walter Savage: the teacher and the story teller

our larger, heavier doors—to the front porch, the courtyard, and the terrace outside the faculty room—keep blowing open and inviting in arctic gusts and drifts of snow. The intercom system has been erratic. Claire Snopek, who left to visit her English relatives on Thursday night, called in this morning to report that she is bedridden with gastroenteritis. We have run out of large denomination coins with which to change the pound notes of students "desperate" to use the telephones to call home.

My inability to get to Oxford Saturday prevented me from getting some texts needed by students who changed their programs late. Somebody—or something, my present primitive superstitiousness insists—has torn the rolled towel dispenser off the Buttery wall. Students are locking themselves out of their rooms every hour on the hour. Dr. Henson's extracurricular riding lesson session on Sunday at a stable in Steeple Aston went off, after a lengthy delay, only because Dr. Henson was able to compress five students and herself into her subcompact Citroen 2 cv. She and the would-be horsewomen macaronically entwined in a groaning, wobbling vehicle resembled circus clowns—all unattached elbows, knees, heads, and bottoms flattened against windows—in the Citroen struggling up the slight incline toward the Abbey gates. (The minibus that the party was to have used was ungettable. The key to the garage door was under lock and key in Reception. The only two people with keys to the basement room in which the garage key was secured were both snowed in in nearby villages. Seagrave also has a key, but he was away visiting his mother.)

As I started the opening sentences of this entry, the wire holding a picture to the Minstrel Gallery wall snapped—was snapped?—and tumbled and clattered onto the mantelpiece, scattering a pile of papers and sending a matchbox car speeding end over end across the floor. The "on off" switch in the laundry room was turned off by...uh,...someone, inducing a mild attack of hysteria in Marilyn Verra and Felicity Hillmer, who had inserted 50p. to do their washing, got nothing for their money, and came complaining to me that "nothing is working here." I resignedly showed them how to turn the switch from red "off" to white "on," but I didn't have the heart to try to qualify their criticism that, normally, I would have regarded as overgeneralized.

At the very moment that they besieged me with waving arms and shrill staccato cries of outrage, I was trying to find a replacement stylus for the record player on which the students are advised to listen, this week, to a *Hamlet* album supplementing their Shakespeare studies. The stylus in need of replacement began to show its age, or bad treatment, last night.

About 7:30 I walked into the game room where the record player was surrounded by seven or eight students, all of them with New Penguin *Hamlet* texts in hand, and all of them mesmerized by the borborygmic growls vibrating the speaker cones: "Arh, dubroo lurb da aroogoo oorf frerm," Hamlet's bowels slowly rumbled while the students, as one, turned their inquiring stares hopefully toward me in a wordless appeal for exegesis. "According to A. C. Bradley," I stated in my best lecturer's tone, my fingertips steepled together in front of my chest, my head tilted slightly backward and my knees thoughtfully bent, "that means that we need a new needle."

I thought that we had completed the necessary steps to get one today, but, somehow my request to Mrs. Raine, the Receptionist, got misunderstood by Mr. Winkler, our engineer, chauffeur, and all purpose maintenance man. We are, consequently, no nearer to producing understandable sound from the record player than we were last night, when Nicholas Baldwin, political science tutor, [and now the Wroxton College Dean] and I tried to transport the only other Abbey player from the buttery bar to the games room.

To make the attempt, we had, first, to go to my bedroom to get the keys to the Reception Office key closet. Then we had to get from the key closet one key to the Buttery and two others for the two locks on the Buttery Bar door. (One is a very old, weapon like implement; the other is a Yale type.) Getting the last two to work agreeably in tandem was by no means simple. They needed much encouragement and flattering from me and from Baldwin, who had a go at the pair of locks after my three minutes of delicate manipulations succeeded, initially, in freeing the top bolt but not the bottom one. Baldwin, in his turn of two or three minutes, was able to coax open the bottom lock but not the top one. When I, thereupon, took painstaking charge of the key to the upper lock while he, simultaneously, soundlessly guided the guided lower one, we finally triumphed, entering the bar with the same sort of joy and wonder that Egyptologists must have felt first entering the tomb of Tutankhamen.

Ours was, however, a fleeting triumph. The cord from the player to plug was sealed into the back of the player. The plug at the other end was at least ten times the diameter of the hole in the unlockable bar framing through which the cord had been passed by whoever installed the rig. Soon after I had to confess my record player failure to the disappointed, and quite clearly contemptuous, students, the one remaining ping pong ball in the games room disappeared. In the midst of my searching for it or another to replace it, Nanette Decea and Stephanie Donato rushed up to ask me to conduct a search of the Abbey, especially the students' bedrooms, in an effort to find out who had just stolen Nanette's Minolta camera. (Ten minutes later Nanette reported that she had found it herself.)

Dr. Nicholas Baldwin, Dean of Wroxton College (1985 - present)

Then there was that trouble with my reading lamps last night. I have two of them on the small chest beside my bed, both of them fitted with 40 watt bulbs. To amplify somewhat the pale amber flow of lumens that falls upon the pages of my late night reading, I balance both lamps on the near side of the chest and tilt their shades up at an acute angle.

About 12:15 I was nearing the final pages of an Edmund Crispin mystery, *Buried For Pleasure*. Like all Crispin mysteries, this one soothed and delighted me with numbers of sections like two that I had paused to smile over reflectively, the book resting comfortably on my sternum. In the first the fetchingly eccentric don/detective Gervase Fen questions Olive and Harry, a pair of rustics who may have witnessed a murder he is investigating.

> "'What did you see?'
> 'We was mollocking,' said Harry…
> 'She'm a rare one for mollocking, is Olive.'
> Olive appeared gratified by this tribute. 'Me Grammer,' she remarked, 'allus says,"When oats be cutting, maids be riggish."
> 'Your grandmother,' Fen tells her, 'is clearly a depraved old woman.'"

In the second, Fen, to recover from the effects of a lengthy scholarly immersion, seeks the distraction of standing for Parliament and seems, unaccountably, likely to win a seat. He delivers a deliberately insulting election-eve speech to antagonize the voters and thus, he hopes, escape sitting in Westminster, an ordeal worse than his recent work on "that malignant poet, Langland." Here is part of the speech:

> "It is often asserted…that the English are unique among the nations for their good sense in political matters. In actual fact, however, the English have no more political good sense than so many polar bears. This I have proved in my own person. For some days past I have been regaling this electorate with projects and ideas so incomparably idiotic as to be, I flatter myself, something of a tour de force. Into what I have said 'no gleam of reason has been allowed to intrude' and I can think of scarcely a

single error, however ancient and obscure, I have failed to propagate. Some, it is true, have cavilled at my twaddle, but their objection has been to its superficies, and not to its inane basic principles, which have included, among other laughable notions, the idea that humanity progresses, and that fatuous corruption of the Christian ethic which asserts that everyone is responsible for the well being of everyone else. Such dreary fallacies as these...have been swallowed hook, line, and sinker. And I am bound to conclude that this proven obtuseness is not unrepresentative of the British people as a whole, since their predilection for putting brainless megolomaniacs into positions of power stems, in the last analysis from an identical vacuity of intellect. What is referred to as the political good sense of the British... resolves itself upon investigation into the simple fact that until quite recently the British have been politically apathetic...It is this which accounts for the smoothness of our nation's development in comparison with the other countries of Europe; and our fabled spirit of compromise...has derived from nothing more obscure or complicated than a general indifference to the issue of whatever controversy may have been on hand; though we, of course, in our vanity have ascribed it to tolerance."

My pleasant progress through Crispin's pages was joltingly halted when my two bed lamp bulbs blew, one shortly after the other. Rather than get out of bed, take off my pajamas and put on a shirt and slacks so that I could go on a bulb snatching foray through the Abbey, I tried to keep on reading by the light of the low wattage of the remaining lamp. (Most of the bulbs here are either 25 or 40 watts. I therefore pushed two lamps together on my side of the bed table.)

After 10 minutes of tilting my head and book awkwardly to get from the dun colored 40 watt bulb the maximum illumination upon my pages, I gave up, doffed and donned and started my late night hunt for a replacement. Luck, or the ways of the Abbey, were against me.

The most accessible room for my bulb raid was #1, just across the small hall outside my Room 2. As noiselessly as possible, I unlocked #2's door and crept in and removed the bulb in the lamp nearest the door. As soon as I got it in my hand, I suspected that something was wrong. When I got back to my bedroom, I found out what it was that was wrong. The base of my bulb was threaded; that on the one that I had just snatched was what is called here the "bayonet" type: instead of threads it had two projections that slip down into grooves in the socket.

Not at all sleepy but unable to read, I turned off the faint amber glow of my lamp and lay in the dark, listening to the cries of owls and the peristaltic sighs and rumbles of the old disagreeable bowels of the Abbey.

The grumbling in the walls was strangely like the garbled speeches of the *Hamlet* record, but in the Bedlam noises I thought I heard the lines "All is not well; I doubt some foul play."

9 March 1985

Saturday

A bright and almost balmy day. Thin scattered clouds drifting south eastward above the heavily mullioned tall windows in my bedroom occasionally filter the strong sunlight. In cool looking waves it alternately washes across the lawn, rises to the dark of the wooded bank by the north wall and then recedes into the angular shadow of the Abbey. (The daylight in my room even on the sunniest mornings has a pale, Edward Hopper quality.)

Somewhere among the lime trees—60 to 70 feet high—and the dense but shorter evergreens, Robert Denton is at work with his chain saw. The growl and whine of the saw cutting through branches reminded me, for some reason, that I wanted to ask him about the wood pigeon feathers strewn in several disordered heaps and patches along the Abbey paths. I hurried out of the building to get to him before he moved off.

Wroxton Abbey casting a shadow on the rear lawn

Formal gardens on the Abbey grounds

Robert put down his saw the instant I came into view. Before I could ask about the pigeon feathers, he entered upon an explanation of his cutting up the tree. "'Twas a healthy tree, but tipped over by the wind," he said, eager to have me understand that he would never have felled it otherwise. "'Twas badly rooted here in a wet spot on the hill. The water gets under them, you see, and the first strong wind knocks them over." When he had finished his comments on the tree, I finally asked him about the pigeons and asked if he, too, had noticed the remains of several.

"Oy," he answered and led me to a place a hundred yards toward the ice house. The soil, covered by conifer needles, was disturbed, and feathers lay in an irregular circle two feet or more across. "Fox has had him," he declared bending low over the spot. "He won't have caught the bird, probably. It will have been `pricked.' The farmers are shooting the pigeons right now to keep them from the seed. Some of the birds get only wounded and fall to ground. Others die in the night and drop off their perch. But oi've watched the fox having a mouse. It's wonderful to see the way it crouches and pounces"—here he rose on his toes and thrust his arms out suddenly—"and comes down right upon the creature."

Robert then asked me if I had seen the badger sett, and, when I told him I never had, we set off on the path north of the Great Pond to the high ground in the woods about a quarter of a mile away. Continuously, as we walked, Robert drew upon his steady and acute observation of the Abbey grounds, proudly showing off his authority as a scholar of the earth. "This would be honey fungus," he said pausing over a pale orange growth on a rotting stump. "Deadly it is. If you get it in your garden it runs right along the roots underground, spreading everywhere and the whole lot is lost." Bracket fungus, he went on, was just about as bad. It got its name from looking like a shelf bracket, he added as a foot-note.

A rabbit started up as we left the stump, and Robert stopped to call my attention to its "form." "They will go underground in a burry," he explained, adding, when he saw my look of slight uncertainty hearing "burry," "We call them `burry' here. Others will say burrow. `Tis all the same," he finished in a tone that left little doubt that the local term was unquestionably the better one. "They keep above ground more now," he said, resuming his remarks about rabbits. "Crafty, they are. They know the fleas in the burries spread myxomatosis." (Robert much admires the ability of wild creatures to perceive all sorts of danger, and, after their form of careful analysis, to draw up reasoned solutions to cope with present threat. Foxes are better equipped for such planning than rabbits, he is certain. "They have moved into urban areas like Banbury," he has told me. "They know they are safe from the hunt there.")

We got to the badger sett only after several more stopovers. During one, Robert pointed to a hole high on the side of one of the tallest trees nearby and told me that it was used by dozens of bats that roost in the rotting trunk. "They'll be in there now. They were once in another weak old beech that we had to cut down. Swarmed out of it, they did, in the light of the morning. This one should come down as well. It will fall soon in a strong wind and will probably damage some of the young trees we've set out for future generations. But I believe we should leave some dead trees about for creatures like the bats. And the green headed woodpecker. The barn owl is almost extinct now, with the way 'modern farming' is pulling down the old barns at such a rate. We need the hedgerows, too, and there are perishing few of them left here about now. I don't think 'modern farms' should be allowed around here. They don't fit in, do they, with their metal sides and roofs and the way they've done for all the spinneys? Every last inch of earth must be plowed. The countryside looks sterile," he said sadly, looking through the trees toward the expanse of rolling hilly farmland, freshly turned over for later "corn drilling."

"I don't hold with squeezing every pence out of the land. If we have enough to live by that's enough, isn't it? Look off there toward Bretch Hill estates. All of that used to be trees. It's horrible looking now, with all the walls and roofs everywhere. And the people don't care for the environment. The young lads come in here with knives and girdle the trees. I will show you some foin' larches and Scotch poins of 30 years or more with the bark stripped off six feet of trunk. There's no point to it. Just vandalism and destruction."

As he nodded his head in mingled anger and despair over the damage to the trees, I recalled a passage I had read years before in Frazer's *Golden Bough* about primitive Germans' love of trees and hatred of those who destroyed them. A typical punishment for girdling a tree, as I recall, was nailing the girdler's navel to the tree and then rolling him round and round the tree, wrapping the barked section with the innards of the malefactor. Studying Robert's expression as he moved away from one of the dead trees gave me a new understanding of the passage.

"Last year," Robert, went on, "was a bad one. They were in the grounds all the toim. Pinched m' favver's tools and pulled stones out of the dam and bridge. A few years ago they stoned the swans, breaking their necks. And one came in wiv a shot gun and blew the ducklings apart. A doozen or two birds, he done for, leavin' the bodies lyin' about. Oi've tried to teach some of the young ones some country lore, but they just give you lip and get ugly wiv you if you try to correct them. `Twill all be like Leamington Spa one day. That was a smashin' place one toim. But it's overgrown now. `Tis all changed, it is. Everything moves too fast. Loik in the States. Coo! That's too swift for me. Oi never get bored with the quiet of these grounds. There's soomthin' new to see and learn all the toim. Even in the winter wiv the snow coverin' all, you can read a great record in the tracks."

Embarrassed, all at once, by recognizing the length of his remarks, he strode rapidly away, neither of us speaking until he drew up again before another hole in a tree. "That there would be a tawny owl's opening," he said.

At another place he touched my shoulder and pointed to a tiny thicket of suckers half a dozen feet above the base of a large beech. He had left the suckers there when he pruned this autumn, he told me, because he'd remembered that a blue tit had four eggs in a nest there last spring, and probably would again this year. Above us a magpie labored upward with a fat stick in its beak, beating its wings strongly and rapidly to clear the top of a larch. I guessed aloud that the nesting would start very soon. "Oy," Robert agreed, "the aconite and snowdrops have been in flower for some toim now." They were all about us in the clearings, the bright yellow butter balls of aconite and tight clumps of spotless white. I looked at them and heard a line in my head: "Numbers of clumps of chimeless bells." I edited it as I followed Robert up the slope to the sett: "Countless clumps of aconite, its golden bells untolled." The punning final word made me smile to myself—out of pleasure or irritation; I couldn't tell which for sure.

The badger sett was well worth the walk. At the edge of one hole Robert scooped up a small, sticky mass of fur, which he separated and let float on the air. It was from a baby rabbit, he informed me, explaining that although only the "rogue" badgers are thoroughgoing predators on game, all of them will "have a yoong rabbit when they can, though earthworms are their steady diet. They find the smallest leverets, he continued, with their wonderful scent, and led me along a badger trail that ran straight to a rabbit's burrow. "They know just where the little ones are. But they can't catch the large ones." He halted me again and stretched the toe of his Wellington, heavily weighted with red mud, toward a small opening in the grass. "That's a bolt hole. Hard to see, they are. Ivery rabbit will have one if it can, twelve feet or more from its burry opening. Sometimes, when you're hunting, you'll see the rabbit rise up by one of these holes, listening and looking for you. If you shoot, you think you've missed sometimes when you haven't at all. The rabbit has plunged down into the bolt hole, wounded. If you take a stout stem of briar, wiv thorns heavy on it, and reach down into the hole, you can often drag the rabbit back out. It got only a foot or two into the run wiv its hurt. That's a little trick that's saved more than one supper for a hunter who knows his business."

Robert pointed out to me several other features of the sett. Some large bones he identified as those of a dead badger, its skeleton exhumed by another one making a later burrow. He picked up a piece of Hornton stone and showed me the marks upon it, proof, he reminded me, of the badger's powerful claws that enable it to dig through rocky soil. A few feet away from the burrow he found evidences of the young badger's testing of their claws by slashing at the bark of a tree. In leading me away from the complex of holes and mounds, he showed me the debris of the badger's old bedding, dragged out of the burrow and replaced regularly with new supplies of leaves and straw. "Badgers are wonderful clean about the burries," he said and reinforced the statement by finding on the surface of the soil a number of cup-sized hollows—"latrines," he explained, in which the badgers void.

Caught up in our walk and talk, Robert went on to guide me around the whole perimeter of the Abbey's 57 acres and beyond, up to the arch by the footpath, over to Trinity College's reforestation plot and then westward to the dovecote and back to the Abbey's front entrance. Enroute, he showed me the carcass of a dead muntjac deer on which "carrion crows" were feeding as we approached. The eye socket, I noticed—and tried at once to forget—had been pecked clean. On the height of a field planted with winter barley, we enjoyed a marvelous view of the villages of Horley and Shotteswell, a prospect, that was, Robert decided, vastly superior to the view of Banbury and the estate houses, semi-detached or in rows of "terraces."

Our walk had taken over three hours. Luncheon was near at hand, and we parted, Robert heading for Wroxton House up the slope beyond the Abbey, I to the cafeteria, where I ran over in my mind others of the items of information Robert had shared with me during the morning. I recalled his regret over the trees killed by the knife wielding boys: "Oi helped to plant those trees when

I was a lad the soize of them what stripped them. Oi got £2 a fortnight for my work then."

Reflection upon his first work for Lord North had led him to a brief impromptu lecture on the history of the grounds: "At one toim the last old lord had about a 100 workers at the Abbey. Near iveryone in the village was in his employ. Twenty five gardeners he had then, and some men just to look after the wall that ran round the whole of the property. There was a water wheel on the stream when I was a lad. It pumped water all the way up to the great house. But it was broken up, along with the house that used to be near. My mother delivered letters to that house on a bicycle when she worked for the postal service. 'Tis a shame they destroyed the dwelling. The Old Lord got too poor to think about repairs. They had to put down some of his dogs near the end, Oi've heard, because he couldn't pay for the keeping of them, and some say he had to sell off one of the farms for £200. When Trinity College took over after his death, they didn't care."

I also remembered his rapt attentiveness to everything we passed. Repeatedly, as we had walked, he leant down and picked up bits of litter thrusting the pieces into a sack to be thrown in the rubbish. Twice he picked up beverage bottles and carried them to where he could bury them under stones that he heaped over them. Once he drew up sharply and picked up a rock fragment four inches square, on the surface of which he had spotted a fossil shell the size of a small thumbnail.

My morning's outing put me in a happy mood, and I decided to cycle into Banbury even though I didn't really have to do any shopping. I just wanted an excuse to be out again in the countryside. By the time I had finished the long climb up

Drayton hill, however, the complexion of the day, and of my mood, changed suddenly. Rapidly massing clouds turned the sunny afternoon gray, and almost at the same time, I discovered that the rear tire of the Abbey bike was slowly but steadily losing air. I also discovered that one of the student users of the bike recently had removed or lost the hand pump I had found attached to the bike's frame just two or three days earlier. Peering over my shoulder every now and then as I pumped my way to the Warwick Road and down it in the direction of Banbury, I comforted myself with the reassuring reminder that there was a petrol station only about a mile ahead.

I shouldn't have counted on it as a source of help. For one thing, the air pump bore a sign warning that use of the hose to inflate bicycle tires was "dangerous and absolutely prohibited." For another, the hose end didn't fit my valve. British bikes come with two different types of valves, only one of them the same size as automobile tire valves. Mine was the other type. I looked for someone whom I could ask for advice but found no one. The station was a self-service one with only a candy selling young woman behind the till. Wheeling my bike away from that station, I saw another one just down the road.

My spirits rose when I saw that it sold bicycles and parts. Its air hose, I learned quickly was of no more use to me than that at the first station, but I approached a young man in the bike department, full of confidence that I would soon be spinning on my way. I wasn't. The young man saw no solution to my problem short of my buying a new handpump and an adapter. My suggestion that he lend me a pump drew from a blank stare of disbelief. He did, however, tell me that if I walked my bike the quarter mile, approximately, to Trinder's on Broad Street, I could get help there.

Pushing the flat tired bike beside me, I made my way to the corner of High and Broad, and saw Halford's bike shop right on the corner. Why go three or four more blocks to Trinder's? I asked myself, looking at the crowd of Saturday shoppers, many of them with enormous prams or leashed dogs trembling and straining to move their sluggish bowels, I went into Halford's, described my needs to a besmocked young man who assured me that the solution was simple and sold me a 60p adapter, telling me that three blocks up on Broad Street, just past Trinder's, I learned, I should find a BP station with an air hose that the new adapter would permit me to use.

A bit sheepish as I hauled the bike past Trinder's, I navigated my way to the station, waited for two car owners to inflate their cars' tires, and then, having with a proud flourish screwed the adapter onto my valve, pressed the end of the air hose to the adapter. Dust rose in a sooty cloud around my head, but the rim didn't. It rested on the squashed tire, unaltered by the rush of air. I tried the hose again, with the same pointless result. Finding no one to ask for help, I rolled the hose back up and pushed the bike back to Trinder's. The clerk there recommend the same remedy proposed by the one in the second service station: buy a bike pump and inflate the tire by hand. "Could I pay you 20 or 30p to lend me a pump?" I asked. "The bike is not mine, and the pump for it is somewhere back in the owner's shed." "Oh. I'll inflate it for you," he responded, and five minutes later—about three quarters of an hour after I had stopped at the first station—I was back in business, rolling the wrong way down Broad Street to the market square.

When I got there and leaned my bike against a wall in the thronged lanes, my spirit changed again. I was certain that no one would bother to steal my bike propped against the wall. All the irritation I had felt in my attempts to get the tire pumped up disappeared. I felt good about being among people so predominantly decent and honest. I finished my chores and headed back toward Wroxton, feeling a mild elation all the way, even though, or perhaps because, the route back is mostly uphill. Struggling up the steep inclines on the old, one speed bike, I felt in the very muscles of my legs and back the contours of the undulating lands Robert and I had looked out over in the shining splendor of the late morning.

A light, brief rain started as I reached the head of Silver Street, just west of the Roman Catholic church in Wroxton. I didn't hurry. I didn't voice any silent hopes that the rain would stop. I wanted it to continue, come down harder. I wanted to be wet, like the leaves of bean plants in the fields around me. I wanted to feel this place on my skin, to be a part of it. When the raindrops ceased a minute or two after the first ones moistened my hot forehead, I felt something like severe disappointment. I coasted down Mills Lane to the Abbey gates, watching the road surface rush under my feet. Was I moving forward, or were the road and the place beneath me speeding away while I stood still, disappearing behind me, flowing into the past? I didn't know. I didn't care.

14 March 1985

It is now 14:45 and the sun is shining brightly. (The self that reads the lines written by the self that writes them is dumbfounded by that embalming opening. But he—or it—can be confidently scornful only by forgetting what today has been like.) From 6:30 or so until 11:00 the sky was full of sun, and the air, though fresh, was clear. At 11:00 gray clouds massed together and formed one thick, low bank of cold mist from which small pellets of frost—not snow—fell in irregular and scattered showers. Then we had a burst of summer sun followed by rain. An hour later we had a proper snowstorm; for about thirty minutes, fat, wet flakes crashed against and slithered down the window panes.

 I watched them for a short time and thought back to my first freshman English class at Middlebury College, convened on a snowy day much like this one, thirty-nine years and 3000 miles removed from this time and place. I remember only one sentence spoken by the instructor, a young man who looked to me then like a cross between Walter Abel and John Lund. He wore socks that did not match and was obviously recovering from some recent heavy drinking that led to his dismissal later in the day on which I met him for the first and only time. Perched unsteadily upon the edge of a table and leaning precariously to one side, he shared with us the riches of his wisdom—or the distresses of his hangover: "As you look out the window at those snowflakes, remember that no two flakes are the same, and none of them ever collide."

I have often suspected that that professorial profundity gave me instantly the courage to contemplate a career as a member of a university faculty: if someone who greets a class with an opening like that one can get a job, why not me? The weight of unworthiness heaped upon me by three and a half years of life in the army as private first class began to lift. (Although I did not know it then, on that winter's shower morning, both my first professor and I were on the move.)

My day today began a bit earlier than usual because I wakened at 6:00, about an hour and a half before the alarm was to ring. I got dressed, experimented casually with the new gym equipment in the basement and then took a walk around both lakes. At the big one I came closer than ever to seeing the munt jac deer. Robert told me last night that he was now seeing them in the morning in the bright red thicket of young dogwoods at the east end of the island. As I came abreast of it, I saw something russet colored flash past a small break in the branches shining in the morning sun. The glimpse was of the briefest sort, however, one of Mark Twain's "candid camera snapshots of frightened creatures in the grass."

I walked on quietly, hoping for another look, but I saw nothing. When I got to the north side of the lake, much closer to the island, I stood motionless for about five minutes, in the hope that one of the deer—Robert said he saw three does and one buck—might appear. None of them did, but I continued my walk certain that tomorrow, or one day soon, I would catch sight of the whole tiny herd. I don't want to leave here having seen only a dead specimen. I want to see one full of life, stamping its small hooves at me, bowing its neck, bounding swiftly away, then stopping for one last backward glance, a mixture of inquisitiveness and blustering but unconvincing defiance, before it springs out of sight.

At the place where I usually end my walk, I cut across the lawn below the gardens to revisit the badger setts east of the sheep pasture that Mr. Fox rents from the College. The side trip was uneventful, but during it I recalled two grim little tales I came upon recently. The first came from Robert, during our hike together on Saturday.

When we got to the top of Taylor's Pool, he broke his silence and said, as much to himself as to me, "Right there," pointing to a distant spot, "is where that young chap from the village fell into the well. He came through the grounds one foin morning, spoke to my dad, and was never again seen alive. He was found later, head down in the old well. We'd hunted a week for him, all through the woods and even in the lakes. The police set up their base in the Abbey for days. They dragged the lakes and even used doivers. And then soombody found him. I've always worried that he may not have perished outright. Terrible thought, him wedged head down that way all that terrible time."

Robert's genre tragedy sent me looking through Kilvert for a passage recounting a similar sort of anonymous rural catastrophe. I found it among his early entries:

"Tuesday, 8 March [1870]. Yesterday there was an inquest at the Blue Boar, Hay, on the body of the barmaid of the Blue Boar who a day or two ago went out at night on an hour's break, but went up the Wye to Glasbury and threw herself into the river. She was taken out at Llan Hennw. She was enceinte [carrying an unborn child]. Met the Morrell children returning from a walk with the first white violets and primroses."

When I came to that last sentence about the Morrell children, I felt, on my second reading, exactly what I had felt on my first: a strange astonishment, a mixture of joy and enchanted disbelief. No highly sophisticated, craft conscious writer could ever have those first three sentences followed by the fourth. Kilvert's doing it is proof of a marvelous simplicity of authorial mind that makes Pepys' or Boswell's most revealing confessions seem subtly calculating. No matter how many times I return to that March 8 entry, therefore, I will feel a warm affection for Kilvert, but also an amusing necessity to make tolerant allowance for his ingenuousness. I will, in other words, feel both condescending toward him and humbly aware of his ability to fashion lines of unforgettable power by accident.

Someone I discussed art with years ago told me that he believed that all great art is an accident. I agreed with him, on the condition that he would agree with me that the miraculous accident befalls only those blessed few who are accident prone. Most of us are too prudential to run the risk of divine calamity.

25 April 1985

Yesterday, I went with Nicholas Baldwin's British Politics class to Parliament. We left Wroxton at 7.30, got to Westminster Palace at 10.20, having been stalled in Lincoln-Tunnel-like gridlock, and spent 2 hours being guided around both Lords and Commons. We also heard a talk by Lord Tordoff, chief Liberal whip of the House of Lords, who had generously granted Nicholas's request that he meet with the Wroxtonians. During the rest of the day (which ran straight through till our 7.30 bus boarding at Trafalgar Square with only twenty-five minutes for lunch,) we sat in on debates in both houses, listened to a talk by Lord Elwyn Jones, a Labor life peer and former Lord Chancellor as well as former Attorney General; watched the Speaker's Procession; and heard talks (in Parliament-building conference rooms) by six different MPs and one secretary to an MP.

The MPs, by the way, were an accurately representative group. Two of them were Liberal, two Conservative, one Labour, and one SDP. They came from districts as widely separated as Truro in Cornwall and Great Grimsby in the northeast.

Tonight I drive a minibus load of modern drama students to Banbury for a performance of *Look Back in Anger*, and tomorrow at 8:30 a.m. I start out with the students for a weekend trip to North Wales. We are to visit Caernarvon Castle, climb Mt. Snowdon, and go on a guided tour of a slate quarry. We will start the return trip to the Abbey about noon on Sunday.

Swan on a Wroxton College pond

We have also had some little excitement and a few busy times on the Abbey's grounds over the past week or so. On Saturday, one of the six swans assigned to us by the "Swan Rescue Association" died. I saw it—it was the cob, the oldest and largest of the parents of four one year old cygnets—thrashing about spasmodically on the water at about 6:00 p.m. By the time I had run up to the village and returned with Robert Denton, the Abbey gardener, the bird was dead, floating with its wings spread on the lake surface and its head and neck hanging like a thick feathery length of rope under the water. Robert and I pulled the bird's body to shore with a grappling hook, fighting off the female, who spread her wings protectively over her dead mate, trumpeted loudly, and tried to frighten us away with thrusts of her bill and noisy, threatening flappings. I thought, sadly, of the old folklore about the pairing of young swans, their gliding together to some thicket-ringed edge of water, touching their heads together—their curved necks forming the shape of a heart, and thus mating for life.

When we carried the sodden weight of the dead male away, the pen began a series of mournful cries that lasted through the night. I closed my bedroom window early, but the sadness drifted in, nevertheless, incongruously mixed, after eleven or so, with the thump and wail of a disco party in honor of newlyweds in the village.

Twice, Robert has had the police in to try to catch a Drayton village teenager who comes into our woods with a fowling piece and begins blasting away at squirrels, rabbits, ducks and swans. At first Robert and I therefore thought that the swan had been shot. A postmortem proved us wrong. He had died of old age or disease, perhaps lead poisoning from dredging in the muddy lake bottom for roots and ingesting discarded fish-line weights or bird-shot pellets. Both are common causes of waterfowl death in England now.

Almost nothing else worthy of comment here, at the moment, is in any way troublesome, but even the grounds can remind you of Wroxton's thought-provoking mix of rustic calm and that which can abruptly astonish. The lawn is greening luxuriantly as spring advances, buds are swelling on tree branches and rose canes, and numbers of the flowers are in bloom. Aconites, primroses, daffodils and jonquils are everywhere in the wooded areas, especially near the ice house on the rise by Lime Walk. Anemone, chinodoxia, and half a dozen other flowers that I know only by sight are brightening the knot garden and the herbaceous borders.

Close to the Folly in the East Garden, however, several shafts of stinkhorn thrust almost lewdly out of the low weeds like ithyphallic totems left over from some Bacchic festival procession. Birds on the Great Pond seem to be responding to this fungus's gamic dehiscence. At least two pairs of mallards are nesting on its banks, and a tufted grebe that everyone concluded last year had been widowed for life has found a mate this spring and is elaborately busy following the rules of a highly stylized and compulsively ardent courtship ritual.

Beyond that, the students are becoming a much more cohesive and thoroughly likable group. I've begun to feel very good about having been able to get to know them. The FDU contingent has been a real pleasure to work with, though their almost aggressive informality seems to perplex one or two of the more traditional English members of the staff.

C. S., for one, calls the tutors "Doll" and gets the attention of her roommate Ellen by whistling through her teeth, piercingly. The other night, she also irritated the chef here by sneaking behind the cafeteria service counter, stealing a second after dinner cream puff, and running out of the dining room. Slim, athletic, and tom-boyish, she easily outdistanced both the chef's cries of protest and the pursuit of a waiter, ordered by the chef to retrieve the cream puff, set aside as dessert for a late-dining staff member. I asked her, an hour or two afterward, to try to set things right by talking to the chef about the incident. She quickly and amiably agreed: "Ok., Babe. No problem. What's the big deal about a cream puff? To tell you the truth, it wasn't worth stealing, anyway."

Her own and her FDU classmates' work compares most favorably with that of representatives of the 12 other colleges from which this term's students have come. And the best grade in the course for which I administered the final, a one point offering called "Britain in the 20th Century," a course that ends several weeks before the others, was earned by a Madison woman, Jill Vacula.

The bells in All Saints tower, not far from my bedroom window, are now tolling, the shouts of the frisbee players on the front lawn are dying down, and someone is pounding on the dinner gong in the Great Hall. It's time to end this entry.

8 May 1985

The students, for the most part an unusually good and congenial group, generate their inevitable occasional difficulties. A man and woman, both of them having drunk more than they should have at our last buttery party, got into a water squirting, beer sloshing quarrel leading to the man's hurling the woman to the floor and bruising her arm. A day and a half of mediation was required to discourage the woman from having her father formally cite the man for assault. The ill will between Mrs. C and every member of the staff over whom my absentee predecessor has given her authority continues to be palpable. It is beginning to surface among the students as well. But there is also here a range of rare and surprising pleasures. The faculty is a joy to work with. They are bright, hard working, and exceptionally cooperative. Conversing with them at luncheon and dinner is exciting and instructive. I will miss them when I leave.

I will also miss the opportunities like two recent ones that Wroxton provided. Last night I led 14 students in the College's "Annual Pub Crawl," driving them in the minibus to 6 different pubs in 4 hours: "The Plough" in Bodicote, "The Saye and Sele" in Broughton, the "Elephant and Castle" in Bloxham, the "Roebuck" in North Newington, the "Red Lion" in Horley, and the "White Horse" right here in Wroxton. Four of them were marvelous old taverns full of beams and timered and pargetted walls and occupied, before my noisy delegation galumphed in, by half a dozen or so locals shooting darts or sitting quietly by the hearth and looking reflectively at their pints of beer or ale.

Our guide for the expedition was Colin Marsh, the sous chef at the Abbey. He obviously knew the territory through which he led us. He gave us previews of each of the places we visited, pointing out that the one to come was a "tied" house whereas the preceding one was "free" and thus did not stock the naturally carbonated ale or beer we had just sampled. Two of my favorites were the "Roebuck" and the "Red Lion." The former left me with two prominent memories: an old man, a faithful local who, according to the woman behind the bar, sat silently in the same spot every night with his pint peering at the fire; and a sign on a massive low beam upon which patrons could quite easily crack their skulls: "Duck or Grouse." The latter introduced me to a fat and amiable labrador retriever with a passion for crisps: he would nose my trousers—with a vilely wet nose—and roll on his back, working all four paws wildly and drooling disgustingly from his lolling tongue until I threw him another handful sized snack.

Although they were public houses rather than true inns, the places we visited brought to my mind a passage in Martha Grimes's *The Man With a Load of Mischief*, dated 1981:

"The English inn stands permanently planted at the confluence of the roads of history, memory, and romance. Who has not, in his imagination, leaned from its timbered galleries over the cobbled courtyard to watch the coaches pull in, the horses' breath fogging the air as they stamp on the dark winter evenings? Who has not read of these long, squat buildings with mullioned windows; sunken, uneven floors; massive beams and walls hung round with copper; kitchens where joints once turned on spits, and hams hung from ceilings. There by the fireplace the travelers of lesser quality might sit on wood stools or settles with cups of ale. There the bustling landlady sent the housemaids scurrying like mice to their duties. Battalions of chambermaids with lavendered sheets, scullions, footmen, drawers, stage coachmen, and that Jack of all trades called Boots waited to assist the traveler to and from the heavy oaken doors. Often he could not be sure whether the floor would be covered with hay, or what bodies might have to be stepped over or crept past on his way to breakfast, if he slept in an inner room. But the breakfast more than made up for the discomfort of the night, with kidney pies and pigeon pies, hot mutton pasties, tankards of ale, and muffins and tea, poached eggs and thick rashers of bacon.

"Who has not alighted with Mr. Pickwick in the courtyard square of The Blue Lion at Muggleton; or eaten oysters with Tom Jones at The Bell in Gloucestershire; or suffered with Keats at the inn at Burford Bridge: or, hungry and thirsty, who has not paused for a half pint of bitter and a cut of blue veined Stilton, flakey

Cheshire, or a knob of cheddar; or known that he would always find the brass gleaming, the wood polished, the fire enormous, the beer dark, the host tweeded, and, upstairs, the halls dark and narrow, the snug room nearly impossible to find—up two stairs, down three, turn right, up five, walk ten paces, like a child playing hide and seek or a counting game? If the streamers have gone from the white caps, and the host is there more in spirit than in fact, like a smile hovering in the air—still with all of this wealth in the vaults of memory, one could almost forget that the pound had dropped." [p. 46 47]

Last weekend—Friday, actually—I went to London with Philip Inwood's art class visiting the Tate Gallery and the National and then going to the theater after having dinner at Wheeler's on Old Compton Road, a block or so away from the theater on Shaftesbury Avenue—quite close to *The Caine Mutiny*, which I saw.

At the Tate I stood for several minutes looking at Hogarth's "The Graham Children," remembering some of the antitheses and balanced contrarieties it has been found to be based upon: in the upper right corner both a cat and smiling boy look at a caged bird, the boy with delighted approval of the song, the cat with a feral, predatory intensity; at right bottom, more or less diagonally opposite from the living bird, a lifeless wooden one lies on the floor; at right top a clock on which is mounted a figure with a scythe points downward to the form of an infant, wide eyed in a world innocent of time and mortality; the infant—as unacquainted with the world's sins and temptations as with the imperatives of time—reaches, with symbolic irony, toward two cherries, forbidden fruit, held teasingly away from her by her older sister, simultaneously child and mock mother; the cherries dangled by the oldest of the three sisters appear as embroidered imitations in the brocaded dress worn by the next oldest; and the sigmoid curves of the draperies and garments contrast sharply with the hard edged zigzags and right angles of floor tiles, frames, and the like.

The portrait is, as well as being the combination of realism and rococo playfulness some viewers have seen in it, an emblem of both the century that produced it and the juxtapositions crowded into the daily life of Wroxton. (Thinking about the contrasts, and oppositions that are a staple of life here at the College, I suddenly recall three facts that right now seem to make extremely good sense: (1) in Warwick Castle's torture chamber display, one notes that the thumb screws are equipped with elegant floral ornamentation; (2) the first slave ship to transport slaves from Africa to Europe was called the "Jesus"; (3) Adolph Hitler played the harmonica. Tangentially, I am also remembering that December 7, Pearl Harbor Day, is the day of the year when the sun sets earlier than on any other day.)

At the Tate, for instance, just after I'd left the Turner collection (to which I'd moved after leaving the Hogarth), I carried in my mind's eye as I entered the men's room, the burst of light rushing through the "Interior at Petworth." The first thing I saw as I came within sight of the water closets was a man dumping buckets of water down the toilet bowls. Perhaps responding to the puzzled look I must have worn as I thought of him at his less that lovely labor a few yards from the Turners, he told me with an irritated shake of his head, "Plug up all the time, the wretched things do. Won't take the great wads of paper people chuck into them as if they was a rubbish tip." And when I got back to the Abbey very late at night and walked down to the laundry room, I heard two women students discussing Ballantyne's *Coral Island* as a possible source for Golding's *Lord of the Flies* while a third woman, too intent upon her efforts to pay the slightest attention to the other two, scrubbed vigorously at the crotch of what are here called "knickers."

Outside my window right now I can see the sheep grazing upon a distant hill while, on the nearer lawn, the gardener cuts the grass with a smoking, rattling gangmower. Life here, in short, exists under the curse of being uncommonly interesting, but I have begun, now, to look forward frequently and keenly to getting back home, to the places and people I especially miss.

19 May 1985

This was a sad day. All of the students left for home. Patty and I felt melancholy watching the last of them go off down the long lane to the village, most of them in a hired coach, but others in groups of two or three in cars belonging to family or friends. Following a policy that has governed many of my days over here this time, I decided to write my way out of the gloominess in which I was wrapped as I walked through the Abbey's suddenly empty rooms and looked over its deserted swards and paths. I sat on the terrace and composed this note to the students:

A FAREWELL MEMORANDUM

Although I will not post this memorandum until after I return to the States on June 1, I am writing it at the Abbey. As I write, Patty and I are sitting on one of the benches on the East Terrace, near the Library windows. It is just after 4:00 p.m., about six hours after the largest group of you left by coach and minibus for London and the airports.

The late afternoon air is bright, warm, and still and full of the calls of woodpigeons, the bleat of sheep, and the final echoes of the bells in the tower of All Saints Church. The sounds seem almost mournful, right now, on this day of leavetakings, and a mood of sentimental melancholy grips those of us who watched you leave. Your departure has convinced some of us staying on here that the Abbey is, indeed, full of ghosts, for we see and hear your spirits still walking the halls of this great old house.

Out of such a mood, I send these lines to thank all of you for your help and friendship during this past term. Life at Wroxton is, sometimes, a social as well as an educational challenge, and I am grateful to you for measuring up so well to both kinds of tests. Patty and I will long remember you with affection and respect. We hope that we can see you again one day back home. Whether we do or not, we wish you well and ask you to call upon us if you think that we can help you.

Roughly two hours after I finished the memo, Patty and I decided to go up to the Wroxton House Hotel for dinner. Blue as we felt when we arrived, we were soon given other things to think about. We sat next to an attractive young English couple and across from a middle aged English husband and wife in a cozy room. Typically for English restaurants, the conversation was quiet, as were the four English diners' use of the knives and forks: every now and then you could hear a stray word and a barely audible click of a utensil. So soft spoken were our neighbors that the splash and gurgle of a waiter refilling a wine glass was a conspicuous sort of clatter.

Suddenly, a party of 15 Americans entered from the bar and took their places at the long banquet table on the other side of our corner table. Most of them carried drinks, and most of them were laughing loudly and speaking to each other in semi shouts. For five minutes or more they argued with one another about the ingredients of a "Harvey Wallbanger." "What's a Harry Wallbanger?" one of them finally asked. "Harvey, not Harry," another corrected. "It's a drink with Gallianos." The two nearest us dropped out of the larger group discussion to call the attention of a third to a bull's eye mirror on the wall. "We had a bull's eye mirror once," the man said. "No we didn't; we thought about getting one," put in the woman beside him in the tones of a wife bored and offended by her husband's consistent mistakes. "What kind of Cha bliss are we havin' with our dinner?" one of the men at the far end of the table asked the headwaiter pouring white or red wine. "Is it dry or sweet?" "Dry, of course, sir," the headwaiter replied, gracefully concealing his astonishment at the question. "OK, I'll have some of the white," the diner answered.

A man two or three seats closer to us told the white wine drinker something about red or white wine—I couldn't tell which because a group between him and me exploded into laughter over a remark by some member of their party about some kind of wine being "bad for anyone with a kidney condition." The young English couple exchanged quick glances and slowly rose and left the room, as did the older pair soon thereafter. I thought suddenly of the way that the pair of cardinals that visit our garden back home darts away whenever a flock of starlings or cowbirds flies in, bickering and chattering.

When we got back to the Abbey it was nearly all dark inside. Piano music, however, eerily filled the Great Hall, illuminated only by the pale gray light of the dying day. Patty and I sat down quietly in the deep shadows, listening. We were not sure who was playing, since the keyboard was hidden from us in the bay below the oriel window. We decided—perhaps insisted, given the stories we had heard about the Abbey's disembodied residents—that it must be Philip Inwood, whose bicycle we had seen parked outside the rear courtyard door through which we had entered the building.

The Great Hall, Wroxton Abbey

We sat almost motionlessly for twenty or more minutes, watching the room darken. The suits of armor on either side of the fireplace steadily lost the lustrous pewter glow they had given off when we first took our seats. Gradually, they became only lighter shadows in the thickening gloom. The music swelled and quickened. The mercury vapor lights on the front porch stair wall flared on, casting onto the ceiling coffers and wall above the fireplace the heavy black outlines of the stained glass armorial bearings in the oriel window. As the daylight disappeared, the black outlines grew increasingly hard edged, sharply defined against the rosy gold light of the porch lamps.

The experience was an extraordinary one. We broke into applause when the music stopped, causing the pianist—it was Philip—to rise in understandable fright and tell us that we had given him a real start. We told him that his music had given us a tremor or two, also, until we succeeded in convincing ourselves that he—that someone—was actually at the piano.

We went up to our bedroom and to bed, considerably lighter in spirit than we had been for several hours. Before I dropped off to sleep, however, I lay quite still, listening to the slow, lower-register kleine nacht music of the Abbey itself: its drawn-out, wood-sounding shudders, its arrhythmic clicks and creaks, and its stony sighs. Then I went to sleep, not unwillingly, but somewhat sadly, groggily aware that my days and nights in the great old house were nearing their end.

29 July 1985

Today, I received a letter from Miss Rina Milsom, of the "Swan Rescue Service," Shotesham, St. Mary, Norwich, Norfolk, NR15 1XX. Miss Milsom is concerned for the safety of our five trumpeter swans, having heard that we allowed several hundred Girl Guides to visit the grounds—and get very close to the swans—just a few days ago, and having learned, also that one of our cygnets has disappeared. She wants us to fence the property and to limit access so that the swans will not be disturbed. If we do not comply, she warns that the Service may have to take the swans away from us. I wrote her this letter:

> Ms. Geraldine Raine has acquainted me with the contents of your letter of 18 July 1985, for which I thank you on behalf of the College. Three of the subjects with which your letter is concerned deserve direct and prompt response.

First, the College cannot consider a fencing project that would be absolutely intruder proof. Our grounds cover 57 acres. Closing the perimeter gaps would be expensive—I would estimate the cost as in excess of £4000—and would require a barrier that would be conspicuously at odds with a plan we are following to restore the Abbey's 18th-century gardens. (The grounds are, of course, regularly and vigilantly patrolled.)

Second, we have had no further news of the missing cygnet. Our groundsman has made extensive enquiries and has carefully searched all the waterways in the area, but he has found no trace of the lost bird. We suspect, however, that it left of its own accord. We have found no evidence of any attack upon it. We will, of course, keep on the watch for our stray, but we have no great hopes that we will find it.

Third, we cannot completely close our grounds to visitors. When we sought grants for some of our considerable restoration projects, we agreed to admit visitors past prescribed times. Though the times of visitation are limited and although visitors are supervised and required to abide by clearly defined regulations, a limited number of people are rather often guests on our grounds. We have not encountered and do not expect to encounter any real difficulty in our efforts to have the visitors and the swans respect each other.

Representatives of your service will always be welcomed as observers of the swans' circumstances and conditions here at the Abbey. If, for any reason at all, any of your observers think that the College cannot provide the birds with the sort of habitat they need, we will, regretfully, agree that the Service should seek a home for them elsewhere. Until we receive such unhappy news from you, however, we will continue to do our very best to ensure the swans' health, safety, and contentment. We have become devoted to them and would sharply miss them were they to leave us.

My duty reminder list for today read like this: Check with the student with the infected foot to see whether or not she needs a visit to the National Health Service. Write to J. Neil Waddell, School House, Bishop's Stortford College, Maze Green Road, Bishop's Stortford, Herts., to ask about the catalogue he is preparing of the C.S. Lewis library. Write—or at least start writing—my recommendations to President Donaldson. Write a press release on Nick's appointment as Acting Director. Make sure that the letter prepared on 7/27 is retyped with all the earlier typos removed. Ask Geraldine about deposits on Newcastle Brown Ale bottles that MBA students take out of the Buttery. Write Tony Baldry, MP for the Banbury district, thanking him for meeting yesterday about the planned Wroxton Advisory Committee made up of local citizens. Write David Luker concerning his complaint about John Seagrave's decision regarding Luker's stipend. Check with Marian Cowie about honoraria for Eithne, Paul, Brian Little, and Tara Heinemann for their work in the MBA program.

Postscript

In the process of clearing out my files and packing up to leave, I discovered a note from a graduate student who assured me that she would send me the text of a "Sound and Light" script about the Abbey—a project that I had suggested to her. Dated "December 10," it reached me several months after I left the Abbey, probably for the last time. Its historical references to the Abbey included this passage about the first layman to own it: "In 1536 Sir Thomas Pope, who was Treasurer of the Court of Augmentations, the ministry responsible for the newly dissolved monasteries and Henry VIII's close friend, purchased the lease to the 3,000 acres of Wroxton manor and land. …he endowed the lands to his younger brother John with the stipulation that John and his descendants hold the lease in perpetuity. Thus, it was Trinity College who collected the income from the property. After three marriages and repeated attempts, Sir Thomas died childless in 1554."v

The incongruous mix of an official, historical tone and the hiccup of solecism in the text set me to reflecting again, with a mixture of mild melancholy and amusement of my own compounding, upon the range of disparities Wroxton has always set before me. My last two or three days there in June of 1985 were a perfect example of them.

Walter and Patty Savage by a pond on the College grounds

Patty and I stayed on after everyone else left except Ron Ward, and he stayed for only one day and night. For at least two days and nights, therefore, we were the sole occupants of the big old house. Suddenly emptied of the staff and students who had made up the community in which we had lived for several weeks, the building seemed dispiritingly chilled and cheerless. It was, furthermore, a far from hospitable place to be. The heat and hot water had been turned off during the nights as part of the shut-down operation. Consequently, whenever we wanted to bathe, we had to get in the tub before 8.00 p.m. or sometime after 8.00 a.m.

Carriage House

North Arms

Hot water for morning coffee required a trip from our Room #2 in the west end of the first floor—American translation, "second floor"—down to the ground floor, eastward to the basement, and through the old cloister corridor from the east end of the basement to the far west end of the oldest underpinnings of the Abbey. In a small, jerry-built kitchen there, we could make use of a two-burner electric stove on which we could heat a saucepan of water, which we would then carry up to our room.

While these circumstances made staying on somewhat grim, they also allowed us the pleasure of having everything virtually to ourselves, and we were able to pretend total and exclusive ownership to the great old building and its grounds, through which we walked in solitude and wonder, only occasionally seeing Robert or one of his parents tending to the beds or clearing brush.

On our very last morning, as we took our final walk past the kitchen by the north end of the Carriage House, Peter, the chef, came hurrying out the door. He was in the midst of a last clean-up of the cafeteria before vacation. He reached out to shake my hand and, remembering his wet hands, wiped his palms on his apron with murmurs of apology. As we smiled at each other in our goodbye handclasp, he said, "Goodbye, sir. It's been a real pleasure to have you in charge here. I think I speak for all the staff in saying that."

His farewell, delivered with great care and a deference that contended with a controlled friendliness bent upon avoiding familiarity, was touchingly simple and sincere. It was also accompanied with an obvious, though far from fully successful, effort at casualness. I found it honestly moving. I thanked Peter huskily through a small lump in my throat and, as I told him how grateful to him and his fellow workers I was for their friendship and help, I looked off toward Lady Lake, partly to break off eye contact.

Over the hounds' cemetery and the path leading to the water a light fog scrimmed the tree trunks and bushes, giving the look of an Oriental landscape to the scene. I felt a sudden urge to leave, to make the departing as short as I could, to put the Abbey behind me. Shortly thereafter, that's exactly what Patty and I did, for we got in our rented car, which we were returning to an agency in Banbury, and began our trip homeward, by train from Banbury to London and then to Southampton and by boat from there to New York.

As I drove up the long driveway to the village, however, I kept an eye on the rearview mirror, watching the Abbey grow smaller and smaller behind us—and larger and larger in memory.

ABOUT THE AUTHOR

Walter T. Savage, professor emeritus of English, came to Fairleigh Dickinson University (FDU) in 1958 as one of the original faculty members at the Florham-Madison Campus.

Born in Haddonfield, Mr. Savage served in World War II and received the Purple Heart when he was wounded in Italy. He graduated cum laude from Middlebury College, Vermont, was elected to Phi Beta Kappa, and was awarded the Reid L. Carr prize for proficiency in English. He earned a master's degree in English from the University of Pennsylvania, and then taught at various colleges before joining FDU.

A well-known and highly respected teacher and administrator, his positions and influence at FDU were substantial: he was chair of the English department; director of FDU's Wroxton College in England in 1966 and 1985; and served with distinction as acting FDU president in 1983-84.

Professor Savage was also a trustee of the Friends of Florham, a group dedicated to the preservation of the Twombly Estate, the site of the FDU College at Florham campus. Professor Savage was one of the most popular professors at FDU, and his dedication was recognized in the many awards he received during his career. He was the recipient of the Alumni Great Teacher Award, the University's

Distinguished Faculty Award for Service, and was named to FDU's Heritage Hall for his instrumental role in the development of the University. He also was awarded an honorary doctor of humane letters degree from FDU in 1984, and later received an honorary doctor of humanities degree from Monmouth University in 1992.

Mr. Savage also had a productive second career as a volunteer. He was a former chairman of the New Jersey Council for the Humanities; and had been a trustee of the

Walter and Patty Savage at an art exhibition during his post-retirement years as a volunteer

New Jersey Shakespeare Festival; Macculloch Hall Historical Museum in Morristown; and former president of the Washington Association. Professor Savage had a second home in Cape May, where he volunteered as a Walking Tour Guide at the Mid-Atlantic Center for the Arts. He was also active with the Nature Conservancy.

ABOUT FAIRLEIGH DICKINSON UNIVERSITY

Founded in 1942 by Dr. Peter Sammartino and his wife, Sylvia (Sally), Fairleigh Dickinson University has grown into the largest private university in New Jersey. Today, more than 10,000 students from 32 states in the nation and 97 other countries are enrolled on the University's two campuses in northern New Jersey and its international campuses in Wroxton, England and Vancouver, Canada. Beginning as a two-year junior college, Fairleigh Dickinson expanded to a four-year curriculum in 1948 to fill the need for higher education in northern New Jersey. In 1954, the first graduate program, a master's degree in business administration, was offered, and Bergen Junior College was purchased as a second campus, in Teaneck. In 1956, Fairleigh Dickinson gained University status and, one year later, the 178-acre Vanderbilt-Twombly estate was acquired in Madison to serve as a third campus (College at Florham).

FDU became the first American university to own a campus in England when it acquired Wroxton College from Trinity College, Oxford University. Opened in 1965, Wroxton College offers American students an array of graduate and undergraduate programs as well as an enriching cultural experience. Formerly a 13th-century abbey, Wroxton College is now a beautifully restored and modernized Jacobean mansion. In 2007, FDU commenced undergraduate classes at a new facility in Vancouver, British Columbia, Canada.

Recognizing that the student profile on most U.S. campuses is changing dramatically, the University's Petrocelli College of Continuing Studies (originally New College of General and Continuing Studies) was formed in April 1998 to provide a unified approach to and enhanced focus on the adult learner and to continue to position FDU as a leader in providing learning opportunities in a strong academic foundation for students of all ages.

FDU has maintained its commitment to broadening global horizons and fostering greater international understanding. In 2000, the Board of Trustees adopted a newly focused mission for FDU: to prepare students for world citizenship through global education.

Each of the University campuses has developed a unique character and vitality. Students benefit from studying at a comprehensive university that offers a wide range of programs and courses, but they also enjoy an atmosphere of warmth and personal attention usually found at much smaller institutions.

Today, FDU offers over 100 degree programs at the associate, baccalaureate, master's and doctor's levels. Its wide range of offerings, coupled with the depth and expertise of its faculty, has Fairleigh Dickinson University poised to serve the citizens of New Jersey and beyond.

Made in the USA
Charleston, SC
31 January 2013